MOBILIZE

MOBILIZE

Strategies for Success from the Frontlines of the App Revolution

Rana June Sobhany

Vanguard Press
A Member of the Perseus Books Group

Editorial production by Marrathon Production Services. www.marrathon.net
Design by Jane Raese
Set in 12.5-point Adobe Garamond

Library of Congress Control Number: 2010936256

ISBN 978-1-59315-645-9
ISBN 978-1-59315-646-6 (e-book)

Vanguard Press books are available at special discounts for bulk purchases in the United States by corporations, institutions, and other organizations. For more information, please contact the Special Markets Department at the Perseus Books Group, 2300 Chestnut Street, Suite 200, Philadelphia, PA 19103, or call (800) 810-4145, ext. 5000, or email special.markets@perseusbooks.com.

10 9 8 7 6 5 4 3 2 1

To the inspired, here is a path.

Contents

Foreword

You've spent months and months on your app for the iPad, iPhone, and iPod Touch, and now the time has come to share it with the world. At this point you'll realize there are hundreds of ways to do this. You could hire an expensive PR firm to spam journalists all day long, buy an ad placed on a mainstream website like *Wired.com,* or start a Twitter account and hope your tweets make their way to the masses. Whatever route you choose, you're going to quickly realize that making it big in the App Store is a major challenge.

It sure seemed easy at first. In 2007, the App Store revolutionized the software industry by introducing a unique business platform where developers both big and small have an equal chance to earn lots of cash. The basic principles are straightforward; all you really need is a good idea, the brains to code it, and the digital street smarts to market it. Sure enough, a lucky few struck gold: independent coder Steve Demeter reported earning $250,000 in a single month with his iPhone game *Trism,* and months later another solo programmer, Ethan Nicholas, raked in $600,000 with his game *iShoot.* Lured by these success stories, tens of thousands of wannabe-rich entrepreneurs have rushed into the App Store with dreams of selling the next blockbuster app. As a result, the game has changed. The App Store is packed with over 200,000 offerings, and the chances of mega success are slim. Digital distribution is a simple and instant publishing model, but making good money? Not so easy.

So that's why you've picked up this book authored by Rana Sobhany. You won't be disappointed. Rana is one of the few people I've met who really gets marketing. She understands that our traditional ideas of product promotion are crumbling in a world that's constantly connected, overflowing with data, and ever changing in the aftermath of the mobile revolution. Just as the App Store opened, Rana launched a mobile analytics company, Medialets. This gave her a glimpse into what makes an app successful, as she networked with some of the brightest minds in tech. More recently you've probably seen Rana making headlines as the world's first iPad DJ, in publications like the *Wall Street Journal, Wired,* and Gizmodo, so clearly she isn't bad at marketing herself either. Rana knows this industry inside and out, and *Mobilize* is a marketing road map to help you hit the ground running.

Reading this book, you'll realize that the Wild Wild West that is the App Store can be tamed with a number of tried-and-true techniques. Rana extracts wisdom from some of the most successful players in this brand new digital frontier: Lima Sky, the now-millionaire makers of the $0.99 game *Doodle Jump;* tap tap tap, a team of brilliant developers who only churn out mega hits; and AteBits, creators of the famous *Tweetie,* which has become the official Twitter app. These developers generously provide guidance every step of the way, from app conception to creation and from submission to promotion. And after your app goes popular, *Mobilize* provides strategies on how to ride the wave for long-term success.

(One additional bonus: You'll get to hear from prickly journalists such as yours truly about how you should and shouldn't pitch apps to the media. We writers are plenty busy, so we're not an easy bunch to sway.)

Of course, this book would feel incomplete if it didn't discuss failures. Poor timing, bad search-engine optimization, and neglectful app "parenting" are just a few examples of practices that lead to a developer's downfall. Fortunately, Rana gets a number of less successful developers to open up about their mistakes so we can learn some valuable lessons.

Make no mistake. Every app is unique, and you're going to have to learn by trial and error what works and what fails for you. But just by reading *Mobilize* you'll gain a sense of direction and, ultimately, an edge over the horde of developers racing to make money in the App Store. With luck, you might even become an app star.

Brian X. Chen
Wired staff writer

Acknowledgments

To my mom and dad, thank you for, well, everything. There are no words to express my gratitude for your love, sacrifice, and support in everything I do and everything I will do. I love you.

To the hundreds of developers whom I've met along my journey in this space, thank you for inspiring me with your vision, talent, hard work, and innovation. I am so honored to be able to work alongside you and call you my friends.

I want to extend a special thank you to everyone at Vanguard Press and Perseus Books Group, particularly Peter Costanzo, Roger Cooper, Georgina Levitt, and Amanda Ferber. You are all incredible and I cannot thank you enough for what you've allowed me to do.

Steve Saffel, my editor, wow. Thank you. I couldn't have done this without you.

To my agent, Lisa Gallagher, you are amazing. We did it!

Brian Chen, Dan Frommer, Matt Drance, Mark Milian, Jenna Wortham, Jenna Landry, Kyle McEachern, Alexis Rodich, Marc Flores, Pete Cashmore, Wilson Tang, Caroline McCarthy, Paul Anderson. I am so grateful for all of you. You've pushed me and encouraged me and now this book is real.

Lastly, thank you to Blue Bottle Coffee, Artichoke Pizza, Pastis, and Virgin America for providing the caffeine, sustenance, ambience, and comfortable seats by which I wrote most of this book.

A Note from the Author

It's rather peculiar to be a veteran of a three-year-old industry, but that's exactly what I am.

In the spring of 2007, we had never seen an iPhone. Isn't that hard to imagine? There was no iPhone. Today, I can't look around without seeing one . . . or more.

I've watched this industry grow and mature from the first minute of its existence. During that time, developers have learned the pros and cons of not only building but also merchandising their apps—and facing the challenges that come along with those tasks. I've sat with developers as they achieved their first million downloads. From a front-row seat, I've experienced the meteoric growth of the App Store.

I have also seen developers screw up, and badly. They listen to advice, nod their heads, and then throw it out the window to do it their own way. Sometimes they've succeeded, but sometimes it's an epic failure.

Yet the beauty of a space that's moving as fast as the mobile world is that the consequences are seldom as dire as they appear at the moment.

I never truly understood the implications of this until I started dealing with ad agencies. These hundred-year-old agencies built their reputations on delivering the best advertising solutions for their clients, and it was really hard to convince someone who established their career designing newspaper print ads that it was worth their time to take a meeting with a three-month-old company specializing in iPhone app ads.

But even back then—when there were five hundred apps in the App Store and the iPhone was a geek device costing $599—we all knew something special was brewing. I was in pitch meetings in which the advertising clients were more excited than the ad agency about the possibilities, throwing out ideas at a fever pitch, with my team frantically trying to keep up in writing them all down.

Now that Apple's iAd has arrived and the mobile advertising field has consolidated significantly; we've seen the results of all those months and years of fighting to prove the beauty of rich media advertising. It doesn't matter how it came to fruition. Apple, Google, Medialets—*who* accomplished it didn't matter as long as the industry was propelled forward. It's an interesting vantage point, though. Now people speak about HTML5 in normal, everyday conversations, but I vividly remember having heated discussions with developers and advertisers who refused to believe that anything but Flash could ever become a standard for ad delivery.

Yet here we are, and here I stand, a veteran of this industry, and everything about this space has changed.

I've spent my entire career learning and leveraging the most cutting-edge platforms, but mobile is different. I have a deep-seated belief that *mobility* is the key to innovation in the future. And we're just getting started. The Web and mobile have followed different trajectories, but in the United States, it's mobile that's about to explode. The stars have aligned. This is not a fad—this is a paradigm shift.

It's not only on the business side of things, either. When I hooked two iPads up to a DJ mixer, it produced the dance beat heard 'round the world. And that's just one example. Every facet of creativity is being touched by the changes that are beginning right here, with iPhone and iPad developers who are gutsy enough to try something new.

———

You bought this book because you want in. It doesn't matter whether you've achieved success on the App Store or if you've never written a line of code in your life. Everyone benefits from collaboration in a space as new as this one.

Over the course of my career I've seen not only the rocket growth of the app ecosystem but also of the people who make them. I've had the pleasure of meeting and learning from some of the best and the brightest. I am consistently floored by the talent and brilliance that exist in the community of iPhone developers. I've said it before and I'll say it again: iPhone developers are my favorite people in the world.

However, I've come to realize that most developers really need help with marketing and positioning.

So this book is my attempt to support the people who make my life richer. In here you'll find interviews with some of the world's foremost developers and a breakdown of the strategies they've figured out along the way. I've structured this book to complete each chapter with a series of exercises that will make you sweat—but to your advantage. And of course, there are such basics as a bibliography and a glossary to help you navigate through the processes and terminology.

I worked really hard to build my company. I slept on a concrete floor for months on end and spent long hours building tools to help developers. I *believe* in this space. I believe in what you're going to do once the fear and barriers of marketing your app are alleviated. I can't wait to incorporate the apps you'll build into my daily workflow. That's what you have the opportunity to do right now. You can actually change how people live their lives. *Plancast* has changed the way I socialize. *SynthStation* has changed the way I produce music. *Flipboard* has changed the way I visualize content.

You didn't know any of these names a year ago.

I firmly believe that the more we can help one another navigate this ecosystem, the greater and stronger the ecosystem will become.

I am available on Twitter (@ranajune) and via email. I am constantly building online resources, and I'll be speaking in person at conferences all over the country about the topics covered in this book. I want you to succeed. Don't be afraid to reach out to me.

It's an honor to serve alongside you as you go through this process.

Love,
Rana June Sobhany

*There's an old Wayne Gretzky quote that I love.
"I skate to where the puck is going to be, not where
it has been." And we've always tried to do that at Apple.
Since the very very beginning. And we always will.*

— Steve Jobs, keynote address, 2007 Macworld Conference
and Expo, six months before the launch of the iPhone

1

The App Landscape

What are your favorite apps?

Ask someone this question two years ago and you'd most likely have been met with stunned silence.

Apps?

What are those?

Today iPhone and iPad applications have become deeply integrated into the way we socialize, run our businesses, schedule appointments, and entertain ourselves. Our mobile phones have become flashlights, tip calculators, and karaoke machines. We use our iPhones to find out what song is being played on the radio, check sports scores and stock prices, buy movie tickets, and remotely access our desktop computers and servers.

The term "app" has become incorporated into our mainstream lexicon to describe any manner of portable software. Apps have also become a currency of cool, icebreakers when engaging in new conversations, and a metric by which someone's priorities are measured.

There's actually a lot you can tell about a person by his or her application preferences.

- Does he have seven pages of apps but hardly uses any of them?
- Does she focus the screen of her iPhone only on her favorites?

Imagine the personality tests that could be developed from these penchants!

The iPhone itself is an amazing device. It was the first widely distributed, mass-market pocket computer—not only a phone but also a camera, a video recorder, a media player, a global positioning system (GPS) navigator, a remote control, and a gateway to email and Internet browsing, all as part of its standard functionality. Every aspect of the iPhone is built for power, style, and utility.

Most important, users *love* to use their iPhones. They love to talk about their iPhones. They love buying cases and add-ons for their devices and defending their choices to naysayers. They will eagerly wait in line for hours to pay Apple for the privilege of owning one.

And one fact remains true about how the phone became the powerhouse it is today . . .

The Killer App Is the App Store Itself

The phone's appeal initially centered around the high-end consumers who were willing to pay $599 for a mobile phone[1] and then brag about it. For them, this object represented the pinnacle of great design; owning an iPhone signified they were capable of appreciating the genius of a device that incorporated a full-featured Web browser, GPS, and all the entertainment of an iPod into a shiny smartphone.

Then as Apple lowered the price and the iPhone began to reach a mainstream audience, the intrigue shifted. The potential emerged for running third-party software that leveraged all the capabilities of the device.

This led to a pivotal day.

Even before the App Store opened for business, Apple had been training users to trust the iTunes Music Store that had opened in 2003. Consumers weren't afraid to hit the one-click "buy now" button in the App Store because they'd already been using it to buy digital music.

Apple licenses from Amazon the one-click technology that makes it hugely convenient to impulse buy.[2] For the better part of a decade users' credit card information has been stored and accessed via one-click. Consumers' innate familiarity with this app distribution mechanism gives Apple a competitive advantage no other platform enjoys.

The launch of the App Store on July 11, 2008, enabled iPhone and iPod Touch users to browse, purchase, and download five hundred different applications onto their devices. They reached these apps via a beautifully designed icon conveniently located on the home screen. The launch of the store opened the floodgates for consumers to experience *hundreds* of independently created applications that catered to many different audiences, for business and pleasure, and for any age group.

They could not get enough, downloading over 10 million applications within the first seventy-two hours.[3] This is the point at which the iPhone became remarkable.

The secondary consequence of the creation of such a robust platform for discovering, downloading, and paying for these applications is that now there really is "an app for that"—Apple's brilliant catchphrase for their App Store campaign. Users know that if they want great content for the Apple hardware, they can rely on Apple-approved software to deliver what they want at the touch of an icon.

A Closed Environment

One of the reasons Apple has been so successful with its product line is that while most digital platforms have shifted to become more open, Apple has remained steadfast around the principle of maintaining a closed platform environment, both for developing applications and for distributing them through the App Store. While this has led to some dissatisfaction and confusion surrounding the rigid and clandestine rules inherent to the application approval system, it also gives Apple full control over the content, design principles, and quality of the applications delivered through their platform.

This makes sense when you think about it on a broad scale and from a consumer's perspective. Whether they know it or not, when consumers download software or music via iTunes, there's a certain quality and aesthetic that permeates the experience. If software were made available through the store that did not live up to this expectation, it would reflect poorly on Apple, not the third-party application developer. And whether you as a developer like it or not, most consumers don't really care who built the application they've purchased, as long as it serves the purpose for which they bought it.

One of the world's foremost experts on all things Apple and iPhone is Brian X. Chen, formerly of *Macworld* magazine and currently of *Wired.com.*

"The iPhone is a closed device running an operating system that is exclusive to the iPhone and the phoneless iPod Touch," Chen notes.

> The major benefit of that is the iPhone has an actual platform—a single immaculate environment for application developers to code in, and a clear audience to target. Other smartphone manufacturers have a messy situation they call "platforms."
>
> With Windows Mobile, for example, Microsoft created a mobile OS that would be shipped with several different types of smartphones made by various companies. Some call this "splintering," others call it "hardware fragmentation." Call it what you will—a complex hardware ecosystem makes it more difficult for mobile developers to sell their apps.
>
> A developer will code an app for an HTC phone, for example, and it's a hot seller there, but maybe only a million of these HTC phones sold last quarter. And then another "hit" smartphone is released, and the developer has to code yet another version of his or her app for another audience of a million or so. That's a lot of work—not to mention digital property—to maintain.

From a developer perspective, it's been economically advantageous to program for the iPhone, despite Apple's questionable and inconsistent approval policy. There's an element of risk with either route, but you're placing a stiff bet in a single circle for Apple, as opposed to spreading smaller bets over multiple circles for other "platforms" such as Windows Mobile or Google Android.[4]

The Mac Developer Community and Culture

One of the defining differences between the iPhone and every other mobile platform is the immediate influx of incredibly well-designed and well-executed applications built atop its platform from day one. One explanation for this is the existing community of passionate Mac developers.

The Mac development community is highly concerned with quality and design, and this may have been one of the driving factors for the first generation of apps built for the platform, even before Apple released the iPhone SDK (software development kit). The indie developer community is tight knit, to the point that competitors often share code with one another in the interest of driving the entire group forward.

"I think Mac developers have brought a certain design sense as well as API [application programming interface] knowledge that allowed them to create complex apps since the App Store opened," iPhone developer Lucius Kwok comments.

On the other hand, some of them may cling to old ways of marketing and selling their apps, and that has kept them back.

- "Cocoa" is one of Apple's application program environments available for Mac OS X, enabling developers to develop apps using tools provided by Apple and other third parties.

- The Cocoa API is incredibly complex and it would take at least a year to learn all the nuances of delegation, memory management, and other details. Without this base of experience, the first apps would have been very limited or would have crashed a lot, but instead we had quality apps from day one.[5]

The *Business Insider*'s Dan Frommer agrees, and notes the advantages inherent to Cocoa:

I think the Mac developer community has been a huge influence on the iPhone. For technical reasons, developers' familiarity with Cocoa; for practical reasons, they already had Macs, which are required for iPhone development; and for spiritual reasons, they were already Apple lovers. Because of that familiarity, they've really cranked up the quality on iPhone apps—look at publishers like the Iconfactory, Pangea, etc.

Although they're probably the loudest whiners when Apple goofs something up, too.[6]

But not all Mac developers feel that the existing community contributed to the success of the App Store. Wil Shipley, founder of two of the most successful indie Mac software companies—Omni Group and Delicious Monster Software—believes that the App Store was so significant on its own that entrepreneurial developers were drawn to the opportunities. Shipley explains:

Certainly Cocoa programmers were hacking apart the iPhone from before the SDK came out, but it appeared the Linux guys were just as active, even then.

When the iPhone SDK came out with the App Store, we saw a huge influx of ex-Windows developers. For example, the number of people attending WWDC [the Apple Worldwide Developers

Conference] went up by a huge percentage—around 50 percent—in the next two years, and it started selling out for the first time ever.

More tellingly, when Apple did surveys of WWDC attendees, they found the greatest percentage of people *new* to the Cocoa platform even after the iPhone SDK came out.[7]

Unique Device Identification

Each iPhone has a proprietary unique device identifier,[8] also known as a UDID, assigned to it. This is one of the most pivotal features of the iPhone from a development standpoint. Unlike other mobile platforms, the iPhone platform gives developers access to the unique code assigned to each iPhone shipped out into the wild.

With the ability to identify specific devices, developers can install analytics into their applications. This then allows them to derive metrics from their applications and understand usage patterns, something that has been exceptionally difficult to do on other mobile platforms.

In addition, iPhone developers can send messages specifically to users who have or haven't taken an action. For example, if you can identify via UDID that a user has downloaded three of your applications and not the fourth, you can set up a prompt to pop up an ad driving the user to install the remaining app.

It's not just the iPhone though. All iPod Touches support application download and usage. So we're looking at more than 120 million devices worldwide whose owners might become your customers.

Not too shabby.

Keep in mind that as of 2010 we're only two years into this platform and that the iPhone is still limited to a few carriers (wireless service providers) globally. (We're not taking jailbroken or unlocked phones into consideration here. Sorry, hackers.)

The future of measurement and metrics on the iPhone platform is up in the air, though. During D8 (Developing 8), the AllThingsD–sponsored conference devoted to media and technology, Steve Jobs publicly announced that he was opposed to the third-party measurement companies revealing data about new Apple products before the products were announced by Apple.

Jobs did, however, express that he wasn't against companies using analytics data to measure ads. It's unclear whether or not Apple is working to create a toolkit embedded in the SDK that would enable metric analysis of app usage. But Apple would be missing a huge opportunity by not pursuing this, and it will be some time before we see the last word on this topic.

The iPhone as a Gaming Platform

One of the early polarizing debates about the iPhone was whether or not it could become a serious gaming platform. On one hand, mobile phone gaming had always been popular among consumers and had consistently been a huge revenue driver for carriers and mobile app developers. On the other hand, incumbent handheld game consoles such as Nintendo's DS and Sony's PSP had had many years to build up passionate user bases and loyal followings.

Yet the rise of the iPhone and iPod Touch has led to a new generation of app users. Unlike players using the DS and the PSP, iOS gamers can download new games with the touch of an app icon, wherever they are.

Developing games for iPhone is very different from developing for other mobile devices. And because there is only one form factor for which to build, it makes sense for game developers to focus their efforts on creating games for the iPhone platform. Developers are able to create robust, beautifully designed games at a fraction of the time and cost of console games. Although the iPhone's retail price is significantly lower, the volume of downloads is high enough to be very compelling to indie developers.

Compared to other handheld gaming devices, the iPhone offers some interesting features that make gaming on this platform arguably more engaging, including geolocation, Internet connectivity, Bluetooth, and touchscreen inputs. While iPhone games are not quite as rich as many console games, Apple and iPhone developers are working hard to close that gap. Developers have even started to create open-source frameworks and toolkits in order to drive the industry forward and provide access to anyone who wants to build an iPhone game.

Of course, the iPhone wasn't the first device to include such features, but it certainly was the first to combine them in a way that makes it compelling for consumers to continuously purchase content. Because the primary function of the iPhone is to be . . . well . . . a phone, users carry the device with them at all times. This is a different modality than carrying around a designated portable gaming console (not to mention a mobile phone, a camera, a video camera, a pedometer, and so on). The iPhone is lighter, more portable, and always readily available because it's always with you.

The trick to creating a winning iPhone game has been creating iPhone-specific gameplay, leveraging features such as the multitouch display and motion sensor to create an experience that cannot be replicated by other gaming platforms. The speed and ease of downloading games via the iPhone's App Store makes it very easy to spend hours and hours getting lost in the gaming experience. The accelerometer and multitouch display make it engrossing in a way other portable gaming consoles haven't even experimented with.

The iPhone has single-handedly caused an evolution in gaming, and consumers are hooked. Plus, gaming has become even more fun with the introduction of features in iPhone OS 3.0, such as peer-to-peer connection and in-app commerce. As Apple continues to make better iPhone hardware and software, developers will continue to make iPhone a preferred platform for which to develop product.

But to lend some perspective, the DS franchise has shipped more than 100 million units and the PSP more than 50 million since both came to market in late 2004,[9] according to a report published in April 2009 by Gabriel Madway of Reuters. Yet even with the significantly higher market share by Nintendo and Sony, iPhone's App Store has already surpassed the DS and PSP in terms of game titles available. When the App Store was just three months old, it offered 1,500 games, while the PSP and DS had about 600 and 300 titles, respectively.[10]

Other companies like Electronic Arts, Sega, and Gameloft are taking the iPhone seriously as a competitor, shifting their attention and dollars to the iPhone platform. Early 2009 brought with it rumblings of a section of the App Store devoted to selling "premium" games.[11] Priced at $19.99, they would feature higher production quality and more in-depth gameplay; they could attract these high-end gaming companies to the iPhone and make it feasible for them to create business units around the Apple platform.

Still, the question remains: is the iPhone a viable gaming platform?

"Without a doubt," iPhone guru Dan Frommer, deputy editor of the *Business Insider,* states.

> It has already prevented me from buying a Sony PSP and Nintendo DS. The most obvious area where it can dominate mobile gaming is casual games. It has better casual games than any other platform— better design, better discovery and installation, and better user interfaces.

And compared the higher-end systems?

> It's also becoming a really cool platform for advanced games, due to several functions working in tandem: High-end graphics, unique interfaces such as multitouch and motion-sensor/accelerometer, easy

in-game payments for virtual goods, and always-on Internet for social and network gaming.

I can't stress enough how important the iPod touch has been for
the development of the iPhone OS as a gaming platform. It's nearly
doubled the overall user base, and has brought the platform into
younger, more-game-hungry demographics much faster than it
would have if it were just the $70/month iPhone.[12]

And the advent of the iPad is just going to accelerate the development
that's already occurring. Though it works in much the same way as
the iPhone and iPod Touch, the iPad's larger screen is going to increase the appeal, and persons who are using this new device for their
book and film libraries are going to want to keep their games just as
available for anytime use. The increased resolution will allow developers to create much more robust gaming experiences with the advantage of also pulling in features such as the accelerometer. In some
ways, this could yield an even richer experience than what's available
on the desktop.

Add to that the fact that there are many emerging companies focusing exclusively on enhancing the gaming experience of the iPhone.
They are creating add-on apparatuses such as external speakers and
game controllers to make it more comfortable to game for extended
periods of time.

From the very beginning of the App Store, the largest category
has consistently been games, averaging between 15 and 30 percent
of applications available for download at any given time.[13] Even *before* the App Store was launched, the most sophisticated and well-
designed applications for the iPhone were games. One pre-SDK
iPhone game in particular, *Raging Thunder,* inspired a generation of
iPhone developers around the possibilities and robustness of mobile
gaming.

But there are some shortcomings not yet resolved in the current
iPhone hardware, including limited processor and graphic capabili-

ties and insufficient memory management. The iPhone is, as the saying goes, a jack-of-all-trades, master of none.

In April 2008, Apple acquired P.A. Semi, a company that manufactures semiconductors such as the ARM chips that will make future iPhones much better gaming machines than they are today by incorporating enhanced graphics and more powerful processing capabilities. Of course, battery life has been a consistent challenge for all mobile handset manufacturers, but with the advent of the unibody MacBook Pro, analysts believe that Apple is working to create a battery that will overcome the strain of hours of heavy application usage.[14] And the iPhone 4 is already showing signs that the battery life of the device is improving, which is great news for game developers and players.

Growing Pains

As early as July 2007—a full year before the App Store launched—developers were building and deploying applications that leveraged all the amazing capabilities of the iPhone. There were incredible 3D racing games, guitar emulators, and VoIP (voice over Internet protocol) applications, all available for free to anyone brave enough to jailbreak their precious iPhone. This covert activity inspired a new wave of developers to examine the possibility of creating software for a mobile platform.

Historically, development for mobile phones has been a long and arduous process, with carriers acting as gatekeepers and success measured by getting "on-deck"—carrierspeak for preinstallation of software on phones before they are activated by consumers. This is a very important distinction, and one that gives iPhone a significant advantage over any other mobile platform to date.

Apple was able to disintermediate the carriers.

For nearly two decades, the opportunity to create and distribute applications at scale on mobile phones had been controlled by the carriers and communications service providers. Pre–App Store, app distribution was excruciatingly difficult for independent developers. Putting aside all the multiple development environments and handset portability issues, in order for developers to get any *real* scale they needed to secure distribution on the major carrier Web portals ("decks").

On the surface this meant lengthy, overly complex, and often litigious negotiations with each carrier on a one-off basis, while behind the scenes the issues governing these deals ended up frustrating even the savviest of salesmen.

Wireless carriers became paralyzed by an identity crisis that in most cases continues to this day. Recognizing that their bread-and-butter, voice telephony services had quickly become commoditized, they struggled to find a suitable replacement on their balance sheets. Not wanting to repeat the mistakes made by the Internet service providers (ISPs)—early winners, then losers, in the Internet revenue pie—the carriers descended into a full-throated embrace of subscription services and/or à la carte pricing models for everything from horoscopes to navigation apps.

For developers attempting free-to-consumer or ad-funded models, this posed an exceptionally difficult challenge. From the carrier perspective, they viewed any "free" app as a direct threat to the "pay-to-play" culture they were just beginning to cultivate in the mobile app space. In their view, they had just finished teaching consumers that in the mobile world—as opposed to online—things cost money, and it didn't matter how much ad revenue the app developer proposed to share with the carriers in exchange for distribution. App-based subscription revenues were dependable and growing, two things Wall Street just loves.

Why risk it all on something as flakey as advertising?

When app developers were lucky enough to get a meeting, the rules they were handed were almost always the same:

- A dictated price point
- A 30%–50% revenue share with the carrier
- A healthy up-front commitment (read: "big cash payment")
- Exclusivity
- Dedicated marketing support (read: "another big pile of cash")
- And a "we'll get back to you" (read: "after we talk to your competitors")

Is it any wonder then that the App Store was such a hit with developers? The tales of woe were everywhere.

"My company built J2ME applications for Samsung phones, pre–App Store," recounts Peter Lee, an experienced mobile developer who is currently developing Google-acquired Aardvark's iPhone application.

> Very bad emulators. Pretty much useless. We had to debug on real phones all the time. Screen sizes are different from phone to phone, so there was lots of screen re-layout. Animations were hard to do. The devices were very limited in memory, so memory management is even harder.[15]

Yet even the rise of the Apple model came with its own detractors. Shazam's former VP of Business Development Kathleen McMahon explains:

> Many developers who came from an Internet pedigree found fault with Apple and the App Store. They were annoyed at delays in the review process, that there was a review process full stop. They were used to hitting one button and, voilà, a Web-style iteration would be instantaneously live. Anyone who lived through the years of "mobile development"—pre–App stores—however, understands the painful slog of yesteryear mobile development: designing for specific devices, platform specification, limitations with the hardware, lack

of access, deeper layer of software, different screen size, etc. It was painful, slow, and resource intensive.[16]

Thus for many, besides being incredibly easy to deploy an application at scale, compared to the mobile carriers, working with Apple is a dream come true.

"People complain about Apple's $99 Dev program," Lee says.

But we have to pay [Internet infrastructure company] Verisign $399/year for a code signing certificate. Apple's Developer program comes with lots of other support. We had a deal for bundled distribution, so our app got to consumers' hands, but that took us close to one year for one app. With Apple's App Store, I delivered seven apps in less than a year.[17]

Large developers like Shazam particularly benefitted from the ease of releasing applications into Apple's application ecosystem.

"The iPhone SDK removed the pain of development," Shazam's McMahon explains.

We had deployed *Shazam* on AT&T, branded as MusicID at the time, and users loved to show off the magic of music recognition. But then their friend might say, "Oh cool, how do I get it?" and the answer was not so simple. Apple made it simple. Not only did Apple provide us with a place to point users to go get it, at the same time that Apple unleashed the creativity of the developer community. Apple worked their own marketing message to put the user's mindset in the mode of thinking, "Gee, I wonder if there's an app for x, y, z." The problem-solving paradigm shift from "How do I get it?" morphed into the now iconic "There's an app for that."[18]

Additionally, due to Apple's sudden shake up of the mobile application space, carriers and handset manufacturers have experienced a surge of interest in mobile apps and app stores (lowercase, of course, when they're not Apple). And yet, carriers have suddenly been yanked from their position of power and dictatorship and relegated to follow Apple's lead. They are now pipe providers, acting as little more than the conduit between the content service provider and the consumer.

While there may be an opportunity to create a scalable business around being a pipe provider, most carriers are reluctant to give up control to a third party. However, in order to maintain control over the ecosystem, carriers and content providers must put infrastructure in place, in order to execute a successful app store strategy—and it is increasingly difficult to justify the spend and resources needed to set up and maintain this framework.

Herein lies the opportunity for entrepreneurial mobile developers to create a real business on the iPhone platform.

App Store 1.0: 10,000,000 Downloads

On July 10, 2008, the day the App Store opened for business, Steve Jobs told Jefferson Graham of *USA Today* that it would launch with 500 applications designed for the iPhone and the iPod Touch. Of the initial 500, 125 applications would be free downloads. (This is a very significant number and will be further discussed in the next chapter.)

Initially, any software built for the iPhone and iPod Touch was referred to as a "third-party application," which in Apple-speak was fundamentally a hedge. In essence it was Apple's attempt to distance itself from these potentially pernicious programs, and as consumers and developers became more comfortable with the platform, "apps" became common nomenclature.

The App Store enabled users to buy applications and transfer them to an iPhone or iPod Touch with the iPhone 2.0 software update, which became available through iTunes on the same day. The applications that launched on the platform ranged from business to game applications, entertainment to educational applications, and many more applications available for free or for sale.

The iPhone 3G, released on July 11, 2008, marked a quantum leap in the capabilities of the device, but not particularly on the hardware side. The new operating system, iPhone 2.0, flipped the switch and enabled users to download and access applications from the App Store.

While there was a significant amount of data suggesting that sales of the new iPhone 3G would be high—augmented by the sight of droves of fans lined up outside Apple, some even camping out overnight—Apple did not or could not anticipate the astounding popularity of the App Store. Up to that moment, it had garnered a great deal of success from being tightly controlled and quality driven. But consumers voted with their attention, and App Store sales reflected an overwhelmingly positive response to consumers' ability to download additional content to their iPhones and iPod Touches.

Ten million applications were downloaded the first weekend. This was staggering to analysts, competitors, and developers alike.

In the month before and the month after the launch of the App Store, I reached out to top iPhone developers and indies alike. I quickly discovered that not one developer I spoke with was actively interested in mobile application analytics—the type of tracking tool that allows developers and sales professionals to understand usage and user patterns. This was especially perplexing to me because I knew that monetization opportunities could arise from having a deep and meaningful understanding of what users liked about applications and how they chose to spend their time engaged with them.

This was a free tool, and yet no one was interested!

The people who *were* interested were drawn in by the price point of the analytics product (free) and really nothing else. These developers weren't thinking about the future of their apps, they were experimenting with a new platform and did not intend to build scalable businesses. For the most part, developers just wanted to build cool stuff.

But everything changed around the end of July 2008. Suddenly individual developers had built applications that had been downloaded 50,000 times.

My phone started ringing off the hook.

"Ohmigod. What are we going to do now?!"

Developers at all skill and experience levels had realized that Apple was providing little more than download figures from customers. There were no purchasing patterns or spending habits. There weren't even engagement times listed—how many minutes a user spent using an application.

This was unsettling to developers who now realized how useful that data would be to them in creating businesses around their applications.

And just like that, Apple reached 1 billion downloads after only nine months in existence.[19]

App Store 2.0: From 1 to 2 Billion Downloads

On July 11, 2009, the one-year anniversary of the App Store, Apple announced that its store had achieved 1.5 billion downloaded applications for the iPhone and iPod Touch. In a press release, Apple CEO Steve Jobs said, "The App Store is like nothing the industry has ever seen before in both scale and quality. With 1.5 billion apps downloaded, it is going to be very hard for others to catch up."[20]

Interestingly, the rate at which customers were downloading apps increased between the milestones of 1 billion and 2 billion downloads.[21]

Meanwhile, Apple's success at attracting developers to its development platform caused a sudden rush by every potential competitor imaginable to attempt to mimic the model. Verizon, Nokia, Microsoft, Google, RIM, and Palm announced development platforms and app stores overnight, all with cute and catchy names. (Except for "BlackBerry App World"—I don't know what they were thinking there. It sounds like an amusement park to me.)

But as other carriers scrambled to catch up, Apple's lead only strengthened.

Savvy developers emerged as clear experts in the field of creating and selling iPhone applications. Veterans of a year-and-a-half-old industry, they began to shape the culture of the App Store, whether they were qualified to do so or not.

During App Store 1.0 many developers were just trying to find out what attracted customers and what was and wasn't working. The residue from these experiments began to color the quality of the App Store. "Fluff apps" saturated the market, and suddenly there was an abundance of $0.99 apps that were of low-value, in terms of both function and design.

Nevertheless, while it had taken Steve Jobs's last big idea—the iPod—four years to become the standard for portable media playing devices, the App Store achieved its benchmark status among mobile application distribution systems in fourteen months. Jobs's belief in the potential of allowing outside developers to develop software for Apple hardware seemed to have been vindicated.

As of June 2010, there were 300,000 apps available to more than 70 million iPhone and iPod touch users in some seventy-seven countries.[22] The iPhone Developer Program has had more than 300,000 participants, and these numbers grow exponentially every day.[23]

App Store's Golden Ratio

In trying to examine the milestones and events that shaped the App Store, I stumbled upon a very interesting ratio. As was mentioned, the App Store launched with 500 applications, 125 of which were

iPhone App Downloads by Date

Date	Available apps	Downloads to date
July 11, 2008	500	0
July 14, 2008	800	10,000,000
September 9, 2008	3,000	100,000,000
October 22, 2008	7,500	200,000,000
December 5, 2008	10,000	300,000,000
January 16, 2009	15,000	500,000,000
March 17, 2009	25,000	800,000,000
April 23, 2009	35,000	1,000,000,000
June 8, 2009	50,000	1,000,000,000+
July 11, 2009	55,000	1,000,000,000+
July 14, 2009	65,000	1,500,000,000
September 9, 2009	75,000	1,800,000,000
September 28, 2009	85,000	2,000,000,000+
November 4, 2009	100,000	2,000,000,000+
January 5, 2010	120,000	3,000,000,000+
March 20, 2010	150,000+	3,000,000,000+
April 8, 2010	185,000+	4,000,000,000+
April 29, 2010	200,000+	4,500,000,000+
June 7, 2010	225,000+	5,000,000,000+

free downloads, giving us the ratio of 75 percent paid to 25 percent free. Despite this imbalance, 75 percent of App Store downloads come from the "free" category.

Even more significant, however, is the fact that 375 were *paid* applications. From day one of the store, developers have erred on the side of charging consumers to download applications. Between the instinctual response to charge for mobile content based on the conditioning from the carriers and—to be honest—the appeal of making money from their software, developers established a tendency to become merchandisers of content.

Which is where the big mistakes started.

Price Points

Now that we've discussed the differences between App Store 1.0 and App Store 2.0, let's talk about the evolution of pricing strategies.

CUE EPIC MUSIC

In the beginning, developers (known colloquially as "devs") priced their applications appropriately. If they felt that their application was worth $9.99, they priced it at $9.99. Then, evil customers conspired against them to lower the price points and deviously schemed to undermine these hard-working devs.

Or that's the story we seemed to be getting from developers who blogged their hearts out about the injustices wrought against them by the evil, evil App Store ("Oh but, PS: Apple, we love you so please don't kick us off your platform! We love you, Apple!").

Give me a break.

An excerpt from a *New York Times* article on July 10, the day before App Store's launch, raises an interesting point:

> Twenty-five percent of the first 500 applications at the store will be free, Mr. Jobs said. Of the commercial applications, 90 percent will be sold for $9.99 or less, he said, adding that a third of the first wave of applications will be games.[24]

In other words, the most popular price point was free. Instead of dictating a uniform price, as he did with music, Steve Jobs let the market decide what price apps should go for

The reality is that developers slowly yet continuously undermined their power to create an App Store they wanted to be part of. Steve Jobs wanted to create a new economy that allowed indie developers to be found alongside the biggest names in gaming and software. A first-time developer tinkering in his free time had the same opportunity to become noticed and successful in the store as did Electronic Arts or Pandora.

How did developers create a mess of the App Store?

It all started with a few developers looking to get ahead, no matter what impact their actions had on the sanctity of the App Store economy.

A History of Cheating

It started out with app names.

Remember *AAAAAAAAAAAAAA Flashlight?* As Apple was struggling to manage the processes of approval, distribution, and marketing for thousands and thousands of applications, a few developers noticed they could leverage alphabetical order to become listed first, with the goal of catching the eye of potential shoppers in the App Store. Apple learned of this tactic and put an end to it within ten days of its onset.[25]

Then developers discovered a gaping hole in the rankings system. This was brought to light when one application, Units Converter, soared from anonymity to the top of the "Paid Applications" list overnight. It was deduced that this happened when an application was changed from "free" to "paid," and all downloads from the period when the application had been listed as free carried over.[26]

So devs quickly changed their price points from "free" to "paid" in order to ascend in the rankings, even though the benefits hadn't been earned appropriately.

Apple put a stop to that gaffe the next day.

But this brings up a bigger and more significant point—that developers have been trying to game the system instead of solve the problem.

This all stems from a fundamental lack of understanding of how to sell. When one is put in an uncomfortable situation where one lacks experience, the result is a biological reaction akin to "fight or flight." No doubt there was plenty of cortisol flowing through the veins of the developer who first learned of the gaping hole in the system that enabled app updates to be considered part of the "New Releases" category.

But these are Band-Aids and, as a community, it behooves everyone to learn the *right* ways to participate in this arena instead of looking for shortcuts.

Apple Didn't See This Coming . . .

The *Business Insider*'s iPhone guru Dan Frommer explains:

> Surely Apple knew that there would be significant interest from developers who wanted to make apps for the iPhone, and from consumers who wanted to install apps on their iPhones.
>
> But it's clear that interest from both sides was overwhelmingly more than Apple expected. And it's obvious the app approval infrastructure wasn't set up right from the beginning. Developers jumped on to the platform because it was technically impressive, because they owned iPhones and could run apps on hardware they already carried around with them, and because of the iPhone's super-simple commerce platform that let them make money from the apps they were making.
>
> Consumers jumped onto the platform because there were cool, good apps, and because they were very easy to find and install. No mobile platform before the iPhone had cool, good apps or had an easy app discovery and installation process.[27]

But with ease and convenience also came scale, and this seemed to happen much more rapidly than Apple's infrastructure could handle. Apple wanted to ensure a basal level of quality for every app listed in the App Store and set out to do this by manually approving each app before it could be available for download. This was—and is—done by a small team of Apple employees whose identities are secret, even to those who work at the company, in order to protect them from malicious or unethical behavior related to the approval of apps.

However, humans make errors.

The application review process has been a recurring sticking point for developers. This appears to be a scale issue more than a process issue.

"The App Store is expanding ferociously, and it's suffering from serious growing pains," Wired.com's Brian X. Chen explains.

> The largest failure for Apple, well-known for its obsessive secrecy, is that the company hasn't yet devised a way to communicate clearly with iPhone app developers and keep them happy. Many complain about poor communication, questionable rejections, and a temperamental app review policy. Apple's closed platform is still the best bet for developers, but it won't be on a long term basis if the company doesn't make major revisions to its app review process. [28]

Adding insult to injury from a developer perspective, Apple's inconsistencies and waffling in enforcing its guidelines, coupled with a lack of clarification when apps are denied approval, has infuriated many developers to the point that they've left the platform entirely. This frustration is understandable, given the big bets developers are placing on the iPhone platform in hopes of building scalable businesses around it.

Still, many developers continue to put up with Apple's controversial application approval guidelines and develop for the iPhone and iPod Touch because the App Store is the most—and perhaps only—viable way for mobile developers to get their applications in front of customers and to generate economic returns from their efforts. Halfway through 2010, Apple finally created a set of guidelines to help developers navigate the approval process. This document can be found within the Apple Developer Portal.

Yet There's No Denying That Something Big Is Happening

Whether or not Apple got it entirely right in setting up an infrastructure and mechanisms for creating an efficient system for application deployment, download numbers and iPhone sales do not lie.

Consumers love applications, and as a result Apple is selling iPhones. Huge media companies like CNN and Condé Nast are launching huge promotions touting how great their iPhone applications are. Giant ads promoting *Popular Science*'s iPad app were all over New York City. Something is changing in the media world, and big players and heavy hitters are taking notice and making moves.

Both Chen and Frommer have very interesting commentary on the success of the App Store over the past two years. "Apple has used the App Store increasingly as a marketing tool for selling the iPhone," Frommer says.

> In the beginning of the App Store, it was one of many features the iPhone offered. Now, it's *the* feature Apple brags about. They wouldn't spend so much money on TV and billboards if it weren't helping sell a ton of iPhones and iPod touches.
>
> It's apparent that Apple has put more resources into the editorial and user interface functions of the App Store. In an effort to surface more of the 100,000-plus apps, Apple has been running more "best of" galleries, including some for holidays, sports seasons, kids, travel, etc., and it recently tweaked the user interface to surface more high-quality apps via the "highest grossing" list. It has become the first must-build mobile app outlet for mainstream—and not-so-mainstream—brands of any genre. Sure, companies were already

making mobile-tailored Web sites, but despite Apple's relatively small market share, innovative apps from non-tech/media companies like Chipotle Mexican Grill, Equinox gyms, MasterCard, and others indicate that mainstream brands are taking this platform seriously.[29]

"It's a matter of setting an example," Brian Chen observes.

Apple is the leader in industrial design, and Steve Jobs is a control freak when it comes to clean, beautiful user interfaces. Those attributes are seen more clearly in the iPhone than any other Apple gadget. The few apps included with the iPhone are gorgeous and brilliantly coded, and they inspire serious developers to code apps with similar quality; some even take the extra step to innovate.

Android and Windows Mobile, on the other hand, do not ship with very inspiring built-in apps, and so developers don't have a great example to live up to.[30]

People Want to Spend Money . . .

One of the most prolific and sophisticated development shops for both the Mac and iPhone platform is Atimi, a Vancouver-based company responsible for bringing flagship iPhone applications to companies such as the New York Times, HBO, DKNY, and NBC to the iPhone. The company's cofounder, Scott Michaels, offers his thoughts on customer purchasing patterns and behaviors:

Consumers absolutely want to spend money, and this is seen in the sales spikes that happen around holidays. App owners see huge gains from gift certificates during the major holidays: Christmas, Father's Day, Mother's Day, and others. Those certificate dollars are spent fast, and iTunes gift certificates have become the plastic gift of choice for so many people. Developers need to take that into account. There used to be a general rule in the software community of offering a free trial for anything over $4.99, but the recent changes to the App Store have changed that.31

Even if the golden ratio—75 percent of downloads come from the 25 percent of applications at the free price point—is true, there are still millions and millions of applications *purchased* every week. These applications have value to consumers, and the smart developers on the platform have figured out how to demonstrate it clearly to consumers. This has yielded big rewards.

But Who Doesn't Love Free?

There's absolutely no risk to a consumer to read a description online, click a button, and install an application. This is one of the benefits of having access to a system as well integrated and simple to use as the App Store. Everyone who owns an iPhone can determine how they would like to customize it, and the beauty of the free price point is that there is no friction in the transaction.

This has given rise to the notion of free trials and "lite" versions of applications in the App Store, and consumers tend to convert well if they are given the chance to try out an app before committing to the full paid version.

> With in-app purchase, now the best plan is to price your apps at free so the users have zero barrier to entry and then target the conversions inside your application, and this is true for many apps [Michaels explains]. The exception is if you are in a niche such as medical devices, in which case you price to the tools you offer, but don't expect the same price you would if you released as commercial software a shrink-wrapped product in the Apple retail store.[32]

Comments and Reviews Are Critical

One of the first actions consumers take when they locate or discover an application they are interested in is to check out the app's rating. This has become a foundational basis for consumer decision making in the App Store and needs to be treated very carefully: it is one of the primary third-party validations of an application for any potential user.

When the App Store launched, anyone was able to review an application, regardless of whether or not they owned it yet.[33] This was particularly dangerous; it led to the pricing disaster we now face, where price compression has scared everyone into a $0.99 price point, regardless of features or functionality.

On October 7, 2008, Apple changed its review policy, and only customers who had *purchased* an application were able to review it. This was a great step forward for the App Store, but it was quickly counteracted by Apple's institution of a new policy that popped up a prompt whenever a user removed an application from their iPhone, asking them to give the app a star rating of one to five.

The problem with that is that someone removing an application is most likely not satisfied. Suddenly the App Store was inundated with one-star reviews with no explanation from lazy or indifferent users who simply wanted to get rid of that annoying pop-up.[34]

Regardless, reviews are really important—*especially* at the launch of an app. We'll talk about this at length in the rest of the book, but here are some key takeaways for app developers:

- Have your friends review your application so the reviews are prepopulated at launch for new and potential customers to see.
- Try to get thirty reviews from your friends and family within the first forty-eight hours your app hits the store.
- If you've launched internationally, you need at least thirty *per store* in each country. The App Store does not share reviews among geographies.

But Commenters Will Behave
as Badly as They Are Allowed To

As critical as positive reviews are for ensuring your application's best foot forward, keep in mind that they can also be your Achilles heel.

It's very easy for your competitors to write negative reviews about your product if they so choose. This is the dark side of marketing that it's better to stay out of, but you as an app marketer need to be aware of what can potentially happen when you create something great—or something threatening to the competition.

And as bad as it is to imagine your direct competitor writing something unappealing about your application, surprisingly, it's the customers you should be most afraid of.

When marketers establish inappropriate expectations for a product in the minds of their target audiences, consumers can retaliate in very unsavory ways. An example of this—which is very common in the App Store—is that an application bills itself as one thing but upon download the user realizes the app doesn't include full functionality, or there are bugs or any of a myriad of reasons leading to customer dissatisfaction. This user is almost guaranteed to write a scathing review, whereas a hundred other pleased customers won't say a word about it.

Even more unsettling is the fact that one negative review can undo the good done by five positive reviews. You must be prepared for this to occur anytime you list a product for sale in a public marketplace.

Where Are We Going?

One of the benefits of the fact that software developers reign supreme on this platform is that most are familiar with iterating to make their product and their processes better and more efficient. Now that we have almost two years of data built up around the App Store and its patterns, we can formulate the best practices and trends around what will work and what won't.

Another type of usage we'll be seeing in the coming months is the rise of subscription-based content. For example, an application itself will be available for free, but can only be populated with additional news, game levels, or content by purchasing them from within the app. As we continue to see users prefer free applications, in-app commerce will continue to mature and flourish.

Mark Milian of the *Los Angeles Times* reports on leading-edge tech and is behind the social media and mobile strategies for that publication:

> When Apple began providing the framework for developers to charge for additional content, it opened a slew of options for apps already out there to create new revenue models and for new players to enter the game with a realistic business plan. For example, the *LA Times* has been looking at the potential of charging for unique features or a new breed of premium content within our app.
>
> From a business standpoint, the App Store and the new in-app commerce model takes a lot of the hassle out of selling things. That's also a win for consumers, who don't have to go through the steps and anxieties of giving their credit card information individually to each seller. Because it's so easy to buy an app, users tend buy more. Two clicks, your credit card is charged and the file starts downloading.
>
> It's easy to get addicted to apps.[35]

This is supported by studies indicating that iPhone users spend more money than other mobile users—not just on purchasing initial applications, but in general.[36] Considering that the iPhone's data plan costs nearly $100 a month, developers know they are reaching a rather affluent consumer just by nature of their owning this device.

The iPad

During the *Wall Street Journal*'s D8 digital conference in June 2010, it was revealed that the iPad was invented *before* the iPhone. When you think about it, the delay in the iPad's release makes sense both strategically and tactically. Much like iTunes served as a primer to train consumers to download and install content onto a portable device, the iPhone got users accustomed to touchscreen computing and applications, so that even before it was released the interaction model of the iPad was familiar and comfortable to users.

Many pundits and critics did not believe the iPad would sell well, but analysts and most of the tech media were rabid for information about the device and how it would be received on launch day. The same lines that snaked around Apple retail stores for the launch of the iPhone were again present for the launch of this new tablet computer, and within thirty days, one million units were sold. By sixty days, there were 2 million iPads in the market.[37]

This was a much faster rate of sale than other Apple—or even any—devices to date, which may mean one of two things: the iPad is transformative to the tablet computing world and will become a mainstream device; or early adopters bought the iPad as soon as it was released and growth will slow and taper off.

Most likely the iPad will be a runaway success because consumers are now addicted to the engagement they have with their iPhones. The notion of bite-sized software that follows a thirty-second-use case scenario makes it irresistible to many laptop users who only use their computers recreationally, or business professionals who may not want to risk carrying their primary machine with them on business trips and to meetings.

The iPad has created a new platform that's very popular, and like the first-generation iPhone it's a high-profile device. The price point is still high and until, like the iPhone, the price drops to a level where price is no longer a prohibitive barrier to entry, owning an iPad gives you access to a very exclusive club.

So is the iPad a large iPod Touch?

That has yet to be seen. People are more likely to use their iPads for entertainment purposes because of the size of the screen. There are interactions possible on the iPad that aren't comfortable or practical on the iPhone, such as watching movies or employing music creation apps. A lot of people like the tablet and enjoy showing it off to everyone around them. It will continue to be a luxury device for the first twelve to eighteen months, however, until the price points fall.

A side effect of the iPad's high price point is that developers are once again charging appropriate prices for their apps. Developers who felt the crunch of the race to the $0.99 price point no longer have to fight price compression, due to the clean slate provided by the iPad App Store. Prices ranging between $4.99 and $19.99 are not only common, but are also deemed acceptable for this device.

This will also cause a new wave of developers rushing to build iPad apps due to the success stories that will emerge as a result of the higher prices. Hopefully, this time around, developers will become wiser and avoid falling into the same pitfall as the last time.

iPhone 4 and iOS

While the iPad's longevity isn't set in stone—yet—two other things occurred in 2010 that are going to change the landscape completely and make possible even more app development than ever before.

During the WWDC, Apple unveiled the iPhone 4, a monster device equipped with a front-facing camera, extended battery life, an improved antenna system, and a gorgeous high-resolution Retina display. Thanks to Steve Jobs's typical presentation fashion, it was impossible not to lust after this new update to the device. But this wasn't as much about hardware as it was about the software that powers it.

Beyond the fourth-generation iPhone, 2010's WWDC also yielded a significant update to Apple's OS strategy. The operating system that powers the iPhone and iPad—iPhone OS—was renamed "iOS," indicating that Apple intends to unify the operating systems for all their devices. In the near future, in fact, there may be one operating system that powers a consumers' phone, music player, tablet computer, television, and desktop or notebook computer with seamless synchronization among them all. Already the new OS allows for multitasking and other features that have historically been lacking, and the cross-platform apps built for the new system will be very impressive.

As a result, there will be an explosion of apps on the market that weren't possible before. Everyone is going to be playing in this space, including the big dogs. This is an opportunity for independent developers to innovate and build products that will become indispensable as the platform continues to grow. The competition will be greater than ever before, so you have to be sure you're doing it right from the beginning, from the onset of your endeavors in this space.

It's up to you to decide how you develop the app, but this book provides the roadmap for what you do *after* you've developed it. You have to make certain your app stands out. You have to be savvy about *everything* in terms of release and marketing of your app.

Think about it . . .

Where are the great success stories lately? In the early days of the App Store, there was an abundance of stories about the Gold Rush and independent developers who, having made millions of dollars, quit their day jobs to develop apps full time.[38] Where are these stories nowadays?

Today, you have to work harder just to have the *chance* to make money with your app. This isn't ever going to go back to the way it was. This is the new App Store, and you have to play by its rules.

The New Rules of the App Store

The App Store will continue to evolve, and participants in this new economy must continuously reevaluate and refine their relationship with the platform. Gone are the days of cheating one's way through the App Store.

In order to create a sustainable platform, we must document and memorialize the best practices that will serve as a guide and template for ensuring high quality on the store. While we can get crafty with our marketing campaigns and techniques—as you will read in the rest of this book—there must be a basal level of understanding for which acceptable practices will be moving forward.

As with all good retail, there are certain rules fundamental to establishing a presence in the App Store. Here are some of those rules.

Rule 1: Remember the Law of Diminishing Marginal Utility

"Diminishing marginal utility" is a law of economics stating that as a person increases consumption of a particular product, while keeping consumption of other products constant, there is a decline in the marginal utility that person derives from consuming each additional unit of that product.

Sounds kind of confusing and doesn't really seem related to the rest of this section, does it? But let's break it down and examine it from a marketing point of view.

This concept boils down to a simple idea: something is only as valuable as what you are willing to pay for it. Thereby, apps are only worth as much as users are willing to pay for them at the time of purchase.

A great example this concept executed poorly is the newspaper industry. The high-level concept of news is that information is very timely, valuable, and accurate. Yet most newspaper content costs less than a dollar to purchase in physical format, and it is absolutely free in digital format. This makes absolutely no sense from a pricing standpoint. If this content is valuable, then users will be willing to pay for it.

As it relates to your app, if you as the decision maker train your customers via pricing strategy that your content is a valuable commodity, it becomes a self-fulfilling prophecy. Inversely, no one wants to participate in content that's *not* viewed as valuable, even if it's only for entertainment purposes.

Marketing your applications well may merit a higher price point, thus increasing the *perceived* quality of your app and leveling the playing field between you and big-name, big-budget publishers. Every developer is an indie developer in the App Store. Everyone is going through the exact same thing.

Electronic Arts values its games at $9.99. Why can't you?

Rule 2: Don't Spam . . . Unless It's Helpful

Many observers say that Apple's App Store download figures and application counts are inflated due to a large number of generally useless applications. This is troubling and devalues the benefits having a closed environment brings. However, moderation of applications via the App Store approval process has inevitably filtered out many of the "test" applications developers are building and attempting to distribute just to say they have an app on the store.

Which brings us to spam. Anytime a developer attempts to game the system in order to advance in the App Store rankings, it is referred to as "spamming."

Spamming techniques have been around since the beginning of the App Store, beginning with the exploitation of naming conventions. And in an effort to drive revenues simply by sheer volume in the App Store, some developers have created thousands and thousands of lightweight shells of applications populated with basic or low-value content, and flooded the market in hopes of tricking a few thousand customers into buying them for $0.99.

To put it lightly, this is not a recommended way to market applications. Apple has started to crack down on this type of behavior. On multiple occasions it has banned developers who abused the App Store platform in this way, eradicating thousands of "filler" applications.[39] But there's a lot we can learn from the spam techniques tested by others that caused users to respond positively. The beauty of a digital distribution system like the App Store is that developers can test pricing, colors, marketing copy, and all other types of branding to determine what users like. Be sure to include this type of A/B testing—comparing your core message with variants to see which works best—when you are launching your application, especially if you think there may be fragmentation in your user base and target audience.

Knowing what your audience wants will help you learn how to best present your application to it in the most appealing way possible.

Rule 3: Avoid Update Fatigue

In previous iterations of the App Store, updating your application was grounds for reentering the "What's New" list, but not anymore. This was a very popular spam technique, but then Apple spotted this trick and quickly changed its mechanisms around app updates.[40] Software engineers tend to be compulsive updaters of their software, but don't assume that consumers are like you. Many users don't know what those red numbers sitting next to the App Store icon on their phone mean, let alone on their desktop version of iTunes.

Update only when you *need* to update. Otherwise you may alienate your core customers.

Rule 4: Don't Necessarily Blame Apple When Things Go Wrong

It seems that the first response developers have when they encounter challenges, no matter what they may be, is to blame Apple. Although Apple has certainly contributed to frustration in some regards, developers have made Apple the scapegoat. This doesn't benefit developers, who ultimately need Apple to provide the platform that has made them so successful.

Developers are constantly getting entangled in the minutiae of their day-to-day experience with the inefficient vagaries of the App Store and neglecting to think about the big picture. Taking a step back, we need to think about the rest of the world and how it perceives the marketplace offering a selection of software to choose from.

"Average consumers could care less if iPhone developers are unhappy," says Brian Chen. Yet Apple has incentive to keep a basal level of peace among iPhone developers.

> The worst possible outcome for Apple would be a developer revolt leading to a mass exodus of famous developers providing killer apps to competing smartphone platforms while boycotting Apple's [he warns]. I highly doubt this will happen, but Apple must be aware there's something broken in its system that could lead to epic consequences if unaddressed.[41]

The first aspect of this rule is that it's not Apple's fault that developers hate the App Store. It seems like every day there's another story about a developer who feels personally persecuted by the App Store's policies. Apple's Phil Schiller, senior vice president of Marketing, has on two occasions addressed this: once when he reached out to prominent Apple blogger John Gruber via email to discuss the decision Apple made in removing a dictionary application from the App Store that contained "objectionable content" in August 2009; and a second time when he went to the press directly to talk about the App Store's approval process in a one-on-one interview with *Business Week*'s Arik Hesseldahl in November 2009.

Chen theorizes:

> Phil Schiller's outreach is hardly a direct solution for Apple's communication problem, but it's a positive sign that Apple is even mak-

ing the slightest effort to publicly communicate its approval process. It suggests the company is aware that it needs to do something to maintain positive relations with developers, and knowing that Jobs isn't the type to sit around and twiddle his thumbs, there must be a larger solution in the works.[42]

And some of the problems are simply the result of the App Store growing so big, so fast. Once again, keep in mind that Apple could never have predicted the level of popularity the store would achieve in such a short period of time.

In order to launch the App Store as scheduled, Apple created a subsection of the existing iTunes Music Store and leveraged existing technology to support the App Store. This distribution system wasn't custom built to accommodate applications, and even two years later many of the basic problems have not been addressed.

For example, consumers can now "gift" applications to one another, which is a functionality that until recently did not exist. Previously, there was an ad-hoc promo code system that was slapped together to enable developers to distribute their apps to the media and other relevant parties. Changes like this are signs that Apple is correcting the challenges for developers. There have, however, been numerous problems with redeeming promo codes for applications.[43] Beta testers will inevitably encounter problems with accessing popular apps if they've recently acquired a new phone or upgraded to a newer model. There is a one hundred–UDID (unique device identifier) limit to beta testing applications, and once you've hit that, that's it.

Early on in iTunes, there was a similar problem on the music side. When users reformatted their computers or bought a new one, the authorization of their new machine would count toward the five computers allowed to play back the purchased content. Apple resolved this—somewhat—by enabling users to purge authorizations once a year and manually reauthorize the machines they wanted to give access to.

Apple has gotten smarter about the App Store, but the App Store still isn't perfect. It will improve as Apple begins to get its head wrapped around the needs and desires of each constituency represented on the platform.

What Does This Mean for You?

Well, first of all, you must have a great idea for an app.

That goes without question. While you can certainly derive strategies and techniques from this book that will allow you to market and sell a mediocre application, that wasn't my intention in writing it. I want to give you the tools you need to strive to build and sell the *greatest* app in your category, and if all goes well, some of the greatest apps in the history of the platform.

Each of us contributes to the current state of the store, and we cannot settle for "okay." As inhabitants of the iPhone ecosystem, our actions dictate the evolution of the space, and until we consider ourselves accountable for those actions, we will be disappointed with the App Store. Even if the idea for your application exists, you must have a unique angle or spin to it—and that might just mean that your app is designed better than the existing ones.

If you can't express how your app is special or different, put down this book and go back to the drawing board.

You must also have the chops to execute it well. If you are building the application yourself and you already know you aren't the best designer, bring someone in to help. If you're outsourcing to a firm, find one you believe can see your vision all the way through to fruition. If there's a financial hurdle, make reinvesting in your application a priority. You only have one chance to make a first impression, but it's never too late to reach your potential.

One of the primary reasons the iPhone has been so successful is that it is so enjoyable and simple to use. If a two-year-old can figure out how to use an iPhone, then we know for certain that interaction design is important. Very important. Build an app that has a fantastic user experience and you will be doing yourself a huge favor. If the difference between two applications is that one is more enjoyable to use than the other, then I can tell you where I'll be voting—with my attention and my purchase.

Claim a Niche

When you're thinking about your application, think about your audience.

Is there a key segment of the population that can become passionate about your application? Perhaps you are building a time-management application. Many different types of consumers—businesspeople, students, parents, etc.—may be in the market for this type of functionality, so plan to tailor your branding and messaging to be the most appropriate for that specific group. You'll be more likely to gain recognition and popularity.

Think about consumer buying patterns when you think about the App Store. Sure, lots of people go to stores to browse, but for the most part, shoppers have something specific in mind when they head to a retail location. Imagine what consumers will think when they see your application.

Was your app designed to solve a problem? Make something easier? You know your application better than anyone. Take a step back and think about it from a broad perspective, and define your value to the market.

Each category of the App Store has a focus that appeals to a certain type of consumer. You must deeply understand the audience you are trying to attract. How do they find out about applications?

Differentiation is key for every application, particularly for one entering a saturated market such as gaming. There must be a unique position to take, and you must think of new ways to separate your offering from the pack. Imagine all the applications that turn your iPhone into a flashlight or tip calculator. At some point, someone decided they would make the *best* flashlight, or the best calculator, and they did it.

No matter how many competitors you have, if you are smart about your industry and understand what your customers are looking for, you can differentiate your offering and teach your customers why they should choose your app over your competitors'.

Build a Great App

I've mentioned this a few times already, but I really want to drive this point home. The best marketing in the world can secure you a download, but it can't earn you a positive review. As an app developer you need to know your audience well enough to create something they will enjoy and *evangelize.*

When you are proud of the application you've built, it shows in every interaction with the media, business partners, and customers. Enthusiasm is contagious, and when you believe in what you're selling, there's nothing more attractive.

As someone who is responsible for constructing and deploying high-end branded applications, Scott Michaels of Atimi offers up his advice for building a great app:

> Aim for half the features you think it should have. Assume the worst
> network signal and CPU speed possible. Make it fast, simple, and
> elegant. The best apps on my iPhone are all exemplary of all three
> of these principles. If you are able to accomplish this, you will have
> the foundation to be able to market and deliver a great application
> on the iPhone platform.[44]

Now let's get down to business. How are you going to sell the application you've spent all these hours building? Are you excited yet?

Yes, a lot has happened in the past two years, and there are more than 300,000 applications available for download in the App Store. Does this mean there isn't any more room?

Absolutely not! The next 300,000 apps are going to be the best ones yet. And every product can have a position in the market, a hook to make consumers not only purchase the app but also believe in it enough to recommend it to their friends.

The next step is *positioning.*

2

Positioning Your Application

One of the primary reasons for writing this book was that I wanted to take the intangible marketing ideas new to most iPhone and iPad developers and make them not only understandable but also *comfortable* to understand. My intention is to take the entire sphere of marketing concepts and focus it, with precision, on how to marry the worlds of software and merchandising. Then measure the hell out of the results to find out what's working—and perhaps more important, what's not.

In this section you will establish exactly how you perceive your app—what you intend for it to accomplish, who your audience is, what they need, and how you will fulfill their needs. In the process you will identify the best ways to spread the gospel, letting them know your app is there, waiting and ready to make their lives richer.

You will also identify your competition, establishing what *they* do for that very same group of consumers. By comparison, you will note what it is that makes your app *better*—an important point you will need to communicate effectively. You will also discover how your competition reaches out to the audience you both covet; you will discover the things they do well and the things they do poorly. And you will learn from both sides of the coin.

Mobilize is a primer to the world of marketing and I am hoping to instill good habits and best practices in a group of people I happen to respect and admire a great deal: software developers.

There are many of you reading this who have worked in some marketing capacity, and you may have your own strategies and secret weapons for attracting attention to your products. If the concepts presented here seem basic, it's because my intention is to set the proper foundation for marketing products in this new ecosystem. My ideas and recommendations are meant to provide a structure and framework that will enable you to be as creative and innovative as you'd like to be. I'm eager to see what this foundation yields and how far you will push the boundaries in the quest to build, market, and sell the next killer iPhone or iPad app.

The iPhone platform, more than any other mobile platform, comes with marketing tools and templates built in that make it incredibly easy to place your product in front of the consumer. *Because* it's so simple to do so, it also becomes easy to ignore the best practices marketers have been creating and refining for decades. App developers simply list their apps and hope they'll succeed. Those who have spent so much time and effort creating pixel-perfect applications blow their chance for success by brushing past the merchandising process.

Don't let yourself become caught in this trap.

From the moment you begin work on your app, also begin to lay the groundwork for bringing it to market. The foundation for the most successful marketing programs is *positioning.* Once you have a positioning statement, that will be the catalyst that drives everything you do to market your app.

But What Is "Positioning"?

From the most fundamental standpoint, positioning is all about placement. In a department store, it would be the physical placement of an object so that the intended audience finds it, examines it, and buys it. So, let's try to think of what this idea means from a marketing perspective.

Positioning as it relates to marketing refers to the process and mechanism for placing a product or idea in a potential customer's mind. It's part art, part science.

First you must establish the unique place your app occupies—what the "big idea" is. That's the *art* aspect of positioning. It's purely conceptual, but it's also essential. Yet there's a surgical precision required to penetrating the noise that bombards your consumers every day, in order to get them to hear *your* message, then make the idea stick and linger. This is where great positioning shines, and lackluster positioning fails to make the impact necessary for success.

Be aware of the potential pitfalls. While the basics of positioning are fairly simple, the stakes are so high that poor positioning can be crippling to even the savviest marketer. Regardless of your skill level, however, you must be courageous with your positioning because to be timid is to appear ordinary. And ordinary products don't typically sell well in any market, particularly not in a crowded marketplace like the App Store.

Positioning has evolved into and emerged as a discrete practice over the past thirty years or so. I first came across the concept of positioning as a marketing weapon when in my college bookstore I stumbled across *Positioning: The Battle for Your Mind* by Al Ries and Jack Trout. The book was published in 1981 but holds just as much weight now as it did then. While Ries and Trout's definition for positioning is slightly different than mine, it's nevertheless very vivid:

> [Positioning is] an organized system for finding a window in the mind. It is based on the concept that communication can only take place at the right time and under the right circumstances.[1]

That last part of their definition is particularly interesting to me:

the right time and under the right circumstances. Does this mean that as a marketer you should sit around and wait for this supposed "right time" to show up and announce itself? Or can you *identify* the proper circumstances in order to reverse engineer the process for taking your killer app to your target audience?

See, now we're getting somewhere.

What Is It That You're Selling?

As you may recall, the first step is to produce a killer app. Once you've accomplished this necessary task, the challenge is to let the world know what you've done.

In order to position your application—or any other goods, products, or services, for that matter—you must have a very clear understanding of what you are trying to accomplish with what you've created. At the core, you need to know *what* it is you're trying to communicate before you can begin planning how you will say it. We'll spend a lot of time here dissecting this process, trying to come up with the right mix of ideas and messages that will stick in your customers' minds.

The fundamental principles of *Mobilize* are based around the work we will do in this chapter, so pay close attention and be brutally truthful—or as they say at Pixar, "necessarily honest"[2]—in the assessment of your product and how it fits in the market.

Where Will Your App Live?

Selecting your venue—in our case the category—for showcasing your application within the App Store is a crucial decision that sets the tone and pace for the rest of your marketing efforts. Where the consumer finds your app determines the first impression you will make.

Thus you must consider the mentality of your customers based on where in the store they will be discovering your app, and layer your messaging around that.

If you are building a music game, for instance, you must choose whether to list your app in the music category or the games category. Each category has its own set of pros and cons and its own set of consumer behaviors therein. Only you can determine which category will provide the greatest opportunity for the success of your application.

Listing a music game in the music category can be misleading to customers who are seeking music creation or music learning tools within that category. However, the apps that compete with yours will most likely be listed in the games category, so being in music might provide a slight competitive advantage to your app.

Ultimately the choice is yours, and only you can know where your app will best fit in. It's up to you to weigh the cost versus the benefit of listing your app in a category just because it may provide a slight competitive advantage. While you may attain small gains, you may also alienate customers who feel they have been misled and subsequently be disappointed by your messaging.

Answering the Question
the Consumer Doesn't Know He's Asking

In my opinion, when positioning is determined appropriately it answers the question consumers didn't know they had yet. For example:

Why can't I live without this app?

Let me clarify this.

Can you imagine your life without an iPhone? Hard to picture, right? Yet for most of your life you had no concept of what an iPhone was or what it could do for you. Indeed, for most of your life the iPhone didn't exist. Even now there are thousands of cell phones out there, but Apple's product was positioned so well, so *compellingly*, that consumers were willing to stand outdoors in lines for *hours*, eager for the privilege of handing over $599.

That's the power of positioning.

The best developers of applications for the iPhone have done a great job of creating compelling explanations of why the iPhone wouldn't be as good as it is without those apps on the platform.

Now think about this as it relates to your application. What purpose does your app serve? How does it make your customers smarter, better, more efficient, happier, or more organized? Think of your app as a solution to a problem, and that will be the key to telling the *right* story about your product.

Once you have defined the fundamental characteristics you'd like to communicate—the ones you *must* communicate if you are to succeed—the next step will be to determine the best way to get this message across. There's a way professional marketers refer to the embedding of these messages within their intended audiences:

capturing mind share.

"Mind Share" as the Holy Grail

In the world of sales, one of the primary forms of measurement—although it's still a rather soft science—is the percentage of market share that has been "captured" by a product: the percentage of the physical retail landscape that product owns.

In the world of marketing, the landscape you need to capture and hold lies within the minds of your audience.

This actually makes sense when considering this notion from within the constructs of my definition: positioning as it relates to marketing is the mechanism for placing a product or idea in a potential customer's *mind*—which is why we as marketers are always trying to acquire "mind share."

If you could measure mind share, it would tell you how many minds your message has infiltrated and left with an indelible impression.

Stay with me here.

Many of the terms marketers use, when taken out of context, sound like posturing, yet they are genuine measures of success when examined for purpose and continuity. I can assure you that "mind share" is very important when bringing an app to market and sustaining its position.

Mind share is properly defined as a measure of customer awareness of a business or brand relative to its competitors. Capturing mind share is typically the means to becoming the leader of the pack, the first step to becoming synonymous with the brand name in a category—and that's the holy grail of branding.

Marketing and all its constituents—public relations, branding, positioning, and so on—start as basic components that evolve over time to form a solid message and structure. Marketing is a lot like painting. You begin on a blank canvas with a base color, then formulate a foundational concept, create a sketch, and then the image begins to take form. At this point it can go in any number of ways, and it is up to the painter to determine what shape it will take.

Mind share as a concept is actually quite fascinating. There are some great and influential books out there that examine it in depth. Chances are you may have read some of them without thinking of them as positioning books. A prime example is *The Tipping Point* by Malcolm Gladwell, one of the most influential business books of the century. Although it was framed as watching the rise and fall of trends, fundamentally Gladwell dissects the *positioning* inherent to some of the greatest marketing campaigns of all time.

One part of the book that really stands out is the case study around the rise and decline of Airwalk shoes. Those shoes were originally intended to suit the needs of skateboarders in Southern California, but the manufacturers wanted to expand into the mainstream market. Realizing there was an opportunity to be positioned as the hip and cool sneaker in the marketplace, the company rallied around promoting this messaging.

It worked. There will always be consumers who want to be considered trendy, and there was a need in the market for this type of niche offering.

But then the company expanded beyond the confines of its original mission and began manufacturing shoes for the general public, thinking *everyone* would want to own Airwalker shoes. In the process they offered a homogenized product that was no longer tailored toward the zeitgeist. This was a misstep that proved irrecoverable for the brand.

Learn from this.

Stay true to your brand. Make your app a talking point by positioning it correctly, and fans will follow.

Think Like Your Customer

Before you can think like your customer, however, you need to identify who your customer will be.

When you set out to build your app, whom did you have in mind? Who *is* your customer?

No, "everyone" is not a relevant audience.

To whom exactly are you marketing your product? With most products, there's a primary group of users who are a perfect fit, and then there is a secondary group. For example, a restaurant guide for New York City is primarily targeted to residents of New York City because they live in the city and will reference it often. However, a huge secondary audience is tourists who visit the city. Each of these two constituencies is reached very differently.

Different types of customers have different needs, and your app will fulfill their needs differently. So the question remains: what value are you providing to each distinct group of your users?

Every person has an emotional connection to a product's characteristics. Some people love quality, others love simplicity. Elegance is often appreciated, but so is complexity—although in software, this trait is better categorized as *robustness.*

What is the reason a consumer should love your product?

We've already established that the App Store isn't perfect, and that Apple has a lot of work to do in getting it to the point where it's the ideal and most efficient platform for distributing apps at scale. But in the meantime, how do customers discover applications in the App Store?

How do *you* use the App Store as a consumer?

Back to the restaurant guide example. Think about where you would reach your two core groups of customers. Where do these users find out about the apps they want? How would you find *your* app if you were looking for it in the App Store?

The App Store is like a mall, so consider the reasons that consumers go to malls. Some people visit to browse, others are there on specific missions, and yet others are simply passing time in a retail environment. The mall experience is different for each of these groups of visitors.

There are different categories of stores in a mall. Some consumers enter the building knowing they are looking for men's clothing but perhaps not necessarily a specific type. They will wander and wander until something catches their eye. They see what they like and step into the store. That's the moment when *positioning* is so critical. If the store isn't laid out in an aesthetically pleasing manner, or doesn't appear to have a selection of merchandise that this consumer wants at a given time, they'll walk out. They may or may not give the store a second chance.

This is exactly the thought process consumers will go through when they come across your application in the App Store.

Now picture a mall directory. It might be divided by category, physical location, or alphabetical order. When you look at this directory, it can help to streamline your understanding of where stores are located, but when you look away from this map, you may become confused and disoriented by the reality of the space you're in.

The App Store is full of so many types of apps, so many titles, and so many price points that it can be overwhelming to the consumer. That's why we have the equivalent of the mall directory—the App Store homepage—to navigate through it all.

Think of all the opportunities a consumer has to walk away from your app. Positioning provides the sparkle that catches a consumer's eye and gets him or her to do a double take when they encounter your app in the wild, whether it's in the context of the App Store, in a blog post, or in advertising.

Don't lose them. If you snag them, you can keep them.

Keywords

Much like the online world needs search engine optimization (SEO), the App Store has its own breed of SEO: keywords. Apple's keywords are a little different than traditional SEO, but then again everything Apple does drips with Apple-ness, and this is no different.

In the App Store, apps are allowed up to 255 characters' worth of keywords. This is up from the 100 characters originally allowed when keywords were first implemented, which to me indicates that Apple recognizes the overcrowding of the App Store. The keyword information you input becomes part of the metadata of your app and cannot be altered until an update to the app is released.

So be very thoughtful about the keywords you choose.

As you do so, leverage the great SEO keyword-recommendation engine Google has put together. Use Google's billions and billions of search results to your advantage in helping you determine what keywords might make the most sense for you to use.

At the same time, check out what your competitors are doing and see if there are lessons to be learned from their strategies. When developers discovered they could list their competitors' names as their own app's keyword, the importance of App Store SEO became readily apparent. This practice was a sneaky way to try to drive search engine traffic to apps, and I suppose it worked for some developers. More than anything, though, it ticked off developers who had worked very hard to establish brand identification and credibility on the store. Now there are firms that offer App Store SEO as a service primarily based around this concept of using other developers' app names.

While this type of behavior may yield short-term results, I can't say that I advocate this tactic. I am much more a fan of building a premium brand around *your* app, rather than piggybacking on someone else's success. If you've built a great app, you won't need to cheat.

The App Store SEO

App Store listings are a significant driver of organic traffic (people who stumble across a product without being exposed to advertising) to applications, and only the apps that have prepared for this discovery channel are able to leverage the marketing platform Apple has provided with the App Store.

Weldon Dodd, a writer with the Apple Blog, has done extensive investigation of search engine optimization in the App Store, tracking specifically the SEO implications of Apple's recent changes in the iTunes preview pages. He has uncovered some very interesting guidelines and conclusions that can benefit developers striving to create compelling and action-oriented App Store listings:

"Customers can only download your app—and pay you if you are collecting money for that privilege—when they get to the right page in the iTunes App Store," Dodd explains.

> There are only two ways to bring customers to this little corner of the App Store where customers can click "buy" and give you the money you so richly deserve. The first method is to click a direct link on the Web—reviews, blog posts, your own site—or in the iTunes store—top apps, featured page, etc.
>
> The second method that customers use to find apps is to *search* for your app, either in the iTunes application or on the Web. Optimizing your app submission to appear in search engine results is critical to your success. You must carefully consider and try to anticipate what customers might search for when looking for something like your app. Keep track of those terms and keywords and be prepared to change them as you learn more about your customers.[3]

When creating your App Store listing, always remember that customers search for solutions.

"When customers are looking for apps, they are looking for solutions to problems," Dodd notes.

> Think about the solution that you provide. Consider the problem that you are addressing. Now use those terms in your marketing

message and in the text descriptions that you use on your website and in the App Store itself.

There are three places in the App Store submission process where you can influence your app's placement in search results. The first two are used when searching inside iTunes. All three are used when searching on the Web. While Web 2.0 names with missing vowels were in vogue not too long ago, you might be better off with a name that is easily understood and rarely misspelled so that the name of your app can spread by word of mouth. Also, the name of your app in the app store is actually more like a title—don't confuse this with the label that appears on the device.

You should load the App title with the keywords you have identified. If you are making a toilet paper tracker—never run out at the wrong time again!—then *TP Buddy* might be a catchy name. It is catchy, isn't it? But it's *terrible* for SEO. The App title should actually be *TP Buddy-the Incredible Toilet Paper Tracker Utility* so that it shows up in search results for "toilet paper tracking," which you have decided is a key search term.

You have 255 characters to play with here, but be sure to use URL safe characters, like the hyphen used to separate the App name from the rest of the title. It seems that using a special character may prevent the words in your title from being used in the iTunes link provided by Apple. You'll still have a link, it will just include your app ID number instead of the app name/title.[4]

Be very mindful of App Store keywords and your app description.

Use commas to separate the terms [Dodd continues]. And remember to use the localization section to specify keywords in other languages, not just English. Apple publishes some helpful guidelines on keywords on iTunes Connect, be sure to refer to these. The best advice here is to avoid terms that relate to the category where your app appears ("utility") and focus instead on the specific terms set your app apart ("toilet paper").[5]

Another marketing opportunity you have is found within the description of your app. You are allocated four thousand characters to provide deeper insight into what your app does and the features it has.

The description is not used at all—at this time—for searches in iTunes [Dodd says]. However, the description appears on the iTunes Preview Web page for your app and is therefore indexed by Google and other search engines.[6]

Timing Is Everything

Positioning should not be an afterthought.

The disaster I have seen time and time again, for marketers of all software platforms—and particularly in the mobile world—is that a team of supersmart developers will come up with a great idea, build a great product around it, launch it, and *then* think about how to sell it.

Say it again.

"Positioning *cannot* be an afterthought."

We can thank the venture capitalists for the abuses of this notion. It's become very common in the technology industry to focus on creating a product regardless of acquiring customers or establishing a proven revenue model. And yet many have successfully raised millions of dollars around their concept with no way of growing it past the first plateau of success. How many billions of dollars have been lost as a result of such actions?

As you may have guessed, I am vehemently opposed to the concept of "launch first, plan later." *Marketing and positioning must be completely integrated into the product planning process,* even if on a very basic level. If you do not identify, plan, and create the mechanisms for consumers to love your product, they simply won't.

You must be calculated with your decisions and prepared to defend your choices if you want to achieve success in the App Store. Certainly, many have gotten lucky with their applications, but as the App Store continues to grow exponentially developers must get a lot smarter about their approaches to the market.

Craig Hockenberry, developer of *Twitterrific* and a principal at the Iconfactory, is one of the foremost thought leaders in the Mac and iPhone development worlds. The *Twitterrific* iPhone app was awarded an Apple design award for "Best iPhone Social Networking Application" in 2008 and continues to be one of the most popular Twitter applications for the iPhone. So when someone like Hockenberry says that marketing is a primary consideration when he builds apps, one would be wise to take heed and follow suit.

Hockenberry explains:

> For *Twitterrific,* we had no idea of what we getting into—we were there on day one of the App Store and have been in the top 10 of social networking since then. No one, including us, knew anything about the market, pricing, customers, etc. There wasn't any marketing process or product positioning. We didn't realize how important that was at first.[7]

The App Store is very different now than it was at launch. Throwing something out to see if it sticks just won't cut it anymore. You can't rely on the luck Iconfactory experienced at launch, and even *they* wouldn't think about doing it that way again.

> Subsequent products have started with positioning as a part of the design process [says Hockenberry]. While brainstorming, the whole team is involved. Once we get the basic ideas in place, a smaller team—about one to three people—refine it. As the design progresses we think about pricing and promotion.
>
> That's one of the revelations of selling to a mass market with iTunes. Marketing is a part of the development process, not something you tack on at the end.[8]

Now that you understand your audience—and even more important, your app itself—you're ready to begin positioning. But before you can jump into the world of marketing headfirst, there's an essential element you still need to develop.

You need to develop a positioning statement.

Cultivating a Positioning Statement

If determining your positioning is the first step, then writing the positioning statement is the next step in the evolution of establishing your product's position in the market.

In Harry Beckwith's book *Selling the Invisible,* he describes the difference between positioning and a positioning statement:

> A position (or statement of position) is a cold-hearted, no-nonsense statement of how you are perceived in the minds of your prospects. A positioning statement, by contrast, expresses how you wish to be perceived. It is the core message you want to deliver in every medium.[9]

In other words, the "statement of position" tells you where you *are,* while the "positioning statement" tells you where you *intend to be.*

To illustrate this, let's use Google as an example. Its position in the market is that of the leading search engine. When consumers think of search, they think of Google. However, Google's positioning statement is actually very different than where it is in the market: "Google's mission is to organize the world's information and make it universally accessible and useful."[10]

When Google creates a mail client or Web browser, they are validating their positioning statement by demonstrating the importance of great user experience across all forms of data and data management. That's exactly what we're trying to accomplish here for your app.

Create a great positioning statement, and you lay the groundwork to make certain your vision can be realized and repeated by those you employ, and even by those who are your customers.

Acquiring mind share means increasing consumer awareness of your product and what your product stands for. This is why a positioning statement is so important. If you're able to effectively and concisely communicate the key values of your application to your core constituency, you can penetrate their perception of your brand and impart the right messages swiftly and efficiently.

Take a minute and think about the brands to which you feel a connection—a *real* connection. Without fail, you'll be able to recite the *reasons* you like these companies and/or what they stand for, without thinking twice. That's one of the key objectives of achieving popularity. It's one thing for consumers to like your brand, but empowering them with the tools to enable them to articulate what you stand for is something else entirely.

So how does this work on the iPhone? It's pretty clear, actually. The companies that have done a great job of positioning have staked their claim to the categories they set out to dominate.

Best streaming music app?
Best Twitter app?
Best use of 3-D graphics?

Each iPhone user has an inclination for an app in each of these categories, and they're not likely to switch their preferences once they've been set.

Personally, I like *foursquare* for my location-based social networking, *Pandora* for my streaming music, *Tweetie* for my Twitter client, and *Camera Bag* for my visual effects. I made these choices at the beginning of the App Store's existence, and in each category no app has been able to overtake them, no matter how hard they've tried to sway me.

Think about the applications on your phone. How did they get there? Was it through advertising? PR? Word-of-mouth recommendation from a friend?

Keep these in mind as you think about the marketing of your own application.

Keep Your Friends Close, and Your Enemies Closer

It's important to realize, though, that there can and should be a lot of competitive companies that play to different consumer mindsets and desires. But in order to get there, those companies still needed to define why they deserved to become someone's favorite application.

Do your homework when determining who your competition is. It's very easy, and even naïve, to think that you don't have any competition. If you really think that, I have to tell you something—you're in denial.

With more than 300,000 apps on the iPhone and iPad platform, it's nearly impossible to imagine there isn't another app that serves a purpose even remotely or tangentially related to what you're building. Now, whether or not that competitor's product is good enough to be true competition is another story, but do your research. Find out every detail about your competitors. Who's on the team? Have they raised money, or are they self-financing? How present are they in the market?

Don't be intimidated by this. The more you know about your competition, the better you'll be able to defend against them.

On the iPhone, developers have the advantage of being able to fully integrate with various features of the device in order to inextricably link themselves to the iPhone experience. Applications like *Shazam* and *foursquare* are two examples of brands that have convincingly tied their application functionality into the unique facets of the iPhone that make it such a compelling one to use. Both have numerous competitors, but both used their understanding of the iPhone to stand apart from the pack and emerge as true leaders in the market.

Be clear about what your app does, and execute against it in the most elegant way possible.

Shazam, one of the most popular applications ever released on the iPhone, enables users to identify the music being played in their current location by touching a button and letting the app "listen" to it. Immediately, the app will ping a server on the back end and display the song title, artist, album name, and a link to buy the music track. Additionally, the app enables users to share their tags (music that was discovered) with friends on Twitter and Facebook, to access the *Shazam* music charts to find out what's hot and recommended.

The developers launched their technology in 2002 and have been mobile focused, leading to the app's use by over 50 million people since then. By utilizing the unique capabilities of the iPhone, *Shazam* has achieved over 35 million users and is considered one of the killer apps.[11]

Shazam was one of the early apps showcased by Apple in its series of iPhone TV commercials, primarily because its developers understood the tools Apple provided to them well enough to build a simple-to-use product serving a very specific need.

Former vice president of Business Development Kathleen McMahon was responsible for leading *Shazam*'s breakthrough success on the iPhone:

> While I am not a technical developer, having had the experience of uploading binaries and doing the actual marketing inputs into iTunes Connect has been extremely valuable and helped shape my strategic thinking.
>
> With that sort of tactical experience, you understand both the limitations and the capabilities to maximize. You also appreciate your developers' skills even more. I am in awe of the developers with whom I have worked. On an analytical level you can understand how they utilize the SDK's toolset, but when they demonstrate their own moments of genius, magically creating user delight, the right brain takes over and you can only say, "Wow, how did you do that?!"
>
> Apple has received praise for building the platform, but Apple has let an entire community of developers stand on its shoulders and receive visibility and reach, including *Shazam*.[12]

foursquare is a location-based mobile application. The type of functionality it utilizes has existed for a long time, but the iPhone has provided an incredible opportunity to showcase how fun—and useful—a game and social application can be on a mobile device.

"*foursquare* is one part friend-finder, one part social city guide, and one part game," *foursquare* cofounder Naveen Selvadurai reveals.

> We wanted to build something that not only helps you keep up with your friends, but exposes you to new things and challenges you to explore cities in different ways.
>
> It's not the iPhone that enabled us to build *foursquare*. So many people can do this on many different mobile platforms. From our perspective, our category of geolocation-oriented apps are easier for

people to understand and more attractive because of the experience of showing them off on an iPhone.

Our app shows you places nearby and where your friends are. It shows you where to go when you're out. It's easy to tell this story with the iPhone. Our app does not necessarily benefit from the hardware perspective of the iPhone because it's a social networking app. Lots of the early adopters see it and download it, and because most early adopters have iPhones, it makes other people want to have it.[13]

But there are some components specifically related to the device that make it an ideal platform to launch an app with.

"[The] iPhone has one of the best implementations of GPS because it is simple and easy to use," says Selvadurai.[14]

foursquare leverages the easy-to-access GPS functionality within the iPhone software development kit to make it the primary selling point of the application. With a few taps on the iPhone screen, users can "check in" to the venues where they are and discover new places and receive new tips about the area around them.

Thus the functionality, when leveraged in a unique and interesting way, can enable users to come up with new ways to love your app. Don't underestimate the power of a passionate user. If you've built an app that users feel is critical to their experience of using an iPhone, the news will spread very quickly and without prompting.

Positioning and Perception

Now that you have a grasp of what the basics of positioning entail, how can you translate this knowledge into something actionable?

The beauty of positioning is that it provides a unique opportunity to define *ahead of time* how you will want to be remembered. A cardboard box can be seen as a present holder, packaging for shipping, a cake transporter, and dozens of other possibilities. How *you* see it depends on how it has been positioned by the person who gave it to you.

The first step to getting your communications program on the right path is to create a clear, defensible, differentiated positioning statement and the key supporting messages that will guide you—and others—along the way as you solidify that position. Long before you have achieved a million downloads of your application, positioning enables you to confidently declare that your app is, say, the best "tip calculator," simply by presenting the facts and reasoning that support such a claim.

Consumers are looking to make decisions, and marketing messages aid them in doing so.

Let's take a moment to think about the concept of perception in and of itself.

Fundamentally, the messages you present to your target audience will be interpreted based on circumstance, delivery, and necessity. Use this to your advantage by recognizing that customers who discover your product wish for it to speak to them in a particular way. There is a certain comfort in owning the *fastest* Twitter client or *best* measurement converter.

It's your job to find out what your audience is seeking.

This is the one area in which you can fake it until you make it true. It's okay to communicate what you're going to be when you grow up, as long as:

- You don't claim your app is something it isn't at all.
- Your positioning statement is clearly where you intend to go.
- You actually intend to go there.

An example of this is positioning based on content that will valuable once it's populated. *foursquare,* for instance, becomes an indispensible social guide once you've added your friends. A Twitter app is only as valuable as the people you follow. Positioning your app as what it will be once the content is present may be acceptable as long as the audience is also informed that there are actions they must take—such as adding friends—before they will be able to gain the full functionality of the app.

If you've done the planning ahead of time, and can genuinely make a compelling argument in defense of your application's merits, your positioning statement should carry you forward to the place you intend to go.

Confidence Is Key

Confidence in your messages, confidence in your products, confidence in your approach. This comes with planning. The more legwork you do in advance of your launch, the stronger your launch will be, and the better your app will be perceived by consumers.

This is critical.

Your fans can only be as passionate about your product as you have given them the tools to be. You have to be willing to stand up for your product, speak about it with conviction, and defend it against others. Beyond the words you pick, this is a type of nonverbal communication that sends the strongest message of all to your audience:

If you aren't willing to be your app's advocate, why should anyone else?

The better and more concisely you can sell your idea, the more likely it is for that message to stick. Particularly in the world of iPhone and iPad apps, consumers love to talk about their favorites. What are they going to say about yours?

Adapt as You Evolve

If you find a message that's working, stick with it until its efficacy wears off and it needs to be revamped. And once it reaches that point, don't be afraid to go back to the drawing board.

Ultimately, when a market reaches a certain size, the participants in that market must step back and examine it holistically. Given the rapid growth of the App Store, even the most experienced marketers and salespeople must evaluate their path and the marketing and product decisions they have made. After you've gone through the exercises outlined below, I wholeheartedly recommend that you go through them again whenever necessary. There's no harm in reevaluating your decisions and iterating based on new and recent data points.

What's the worst that could happen?

You could make more money, or make your customers happier, or solidify your position in the marketplace?

Your Positioning Statement

What are the most urgent and unique facets of your company?

What is the *one sentence* that encapsulates all these ideas into a call to action that makes it impossible for a potential customer not to fall in love with you immediately?

We've already discussed that Google's mission statement is "to organize the world's information and make it universally accessible and useful." How about a few other examples?

Coca-Cola's promise is to "benefit and refresh everyone it touches."[15]

Amazon.com's mission statement is "to build a place where people can come to find and discover anything they might want to buy online."[16]

What about you?

Take a shot at it. You'll have another chance at the end of this chapter to revise it if you aren't satisfied with your first attempt.

My product is _____. It does _____ in a way no other app can by _____.

Positioning Workout for First-Time Marketers

This is where you really begin to build your marketing muscle.

The next section will be a workbook for you to create your product's position. You will need to commit to this section and work hard on filling out the following questions. Some of the topics were addressed in this chapter; others will unfold in the next.

Be honest with yourself. This is the foundation for how to market. You cannot afford to be under the illusion that you have no competitors and that your approach is perfect. By being critical with yourself you will grow as a marketer.

Take negatives and spin them to make them positive. Each member of your team should answer the questions independently, without consulting others for opinions. The cumulative answers will provide a robust and comprehensive overview of all the facets of your app's position.

What does your app do?

_____

_____

_____

_____

_____

_____

_____

_____

_____

What does your app do better than anyone else's?

_____

_____

_____

_____

_____
_____
_____
_____
_____
_____

What are the most memorable aspects of your app?

_____
_____
_____
_____
_____
_____
_____
_____
_____

In what category of the App Store will your product live?

_____
_____
_____

What are the key attributes of that section? Think about the other apps listed there, as well as what customers expect when they go there.

_____
_____
_____
_____
_____
_____
_____
_____
_____

Ideally, what will your customers experience when they engage with and/or experience your app for the first time?

_____

_____

_____

_____

_____

_____

_____

_____

_____

Who are your core customers? In other words, who are the main group of people who will be looking for and ultimately downloading your app?

_____

_____

_____

_____

_____

_____

_____

_____

_____

What are their characteristics (including income, age, and gender)?

_____

_____

_____

_____

_____

_____

_____

_____

Why do these customers need your products?

_____

_____

_____

_____

_____

_____

_____

_____

_____

How do they find out about the products they acquire?

_____

_____

_____

_____

_____

_____

_____

_____

_____

How can you reach your primary audience?

_____

_____

_____

_____

_____

_____

_____

_____

_____

Who are your secondary customers? Who are the next group of people in line to download your app—the ones who don't yet know they need it?

_____

_____

_____

_____

_____

_____

_____

_____

_____

_____

What are their characteristics?

_____

_____

_____

_____

_____

_____

_____

_____

Why do these customers need your products?

_____

_____

_____

_____

_____

_____

_____

_____

_____

How do they find information? Blogs? Newspapers? Word of mouth?

_____

_____

_____

_____

_____

_____

_____

_____

_____

How can you reach your secondary audience?

_____

_____

_____

_____

_____

_____

_____

_____

_____

What benefits do your customers receive by downloading your app?

_____

_____

_____

_____

_____

_____

_____

_____

_____

What words or phrases would you like to have associated with your app?

_____

_____

_____

_____

_____

_____

_____

_____

What words or phrases would you not like to have associated with your app?

_____

_____

_____

_____

_____

_____

_____

Are there any overlaps between these two previous answers that will hinder your ability to have consumers think about your app the way you'd like them to? (That is, you want them to think it's a fast app, but in reality it is laggy. You need to address genuine problems with the app, as well as perception problems.)

_____

_____

_____

_____

_____

_____

_____

_____

Who are your competitors?

_____
_____
_____
_____
_____
_____
_____
_____
_____

What are your competitors doing successfully to reach their core audiences?

_____
_____
_____
_____
_____
_____
_____
_____
_____

What are your competitors doing right?

_____
_____
_____
_____
_____
_____
_____
_____
_____

What are your competitors doing wrong?

_____

_____

_____

_____

_____

_____

_____

_____

What are the lessons you can learn that you can exploit for marketing purposes or from a messaging standpoint?

_____

_____

_____

_____

_____

_____

_____

_____

_____

What will it take to make your vision a reality? List individual components, whether they are in your control or not.

_____

_____

_____

_____

_____

_____

_____

_____

_____

_____

Consider these answers the blank canvas I mentioned earlier, on which you'll be painting your masterpiece.

There is a unique feeling an entrepreneur gets from reading the *right* positioning statement. It feels right. It feels like a plan. If you don't feel that, do this exercise over again until you're left with the message you feel exemplifies your vision.

We've successfully identified your value to your customers, how they will discover you, and why they will love you. From this foundation, we will now refine these things into a simple, straightforward, and concise sentence that encapsulates the core of your product's position. This will then be used anywhere your product is described:

- In the App Store listings
- On your product website
- In sales presentations
- In press interviews

Remember that a brand is built through the consistency of its messages.

Take all your answers, put them in a safe place, and go to sleep. When you wake up, review them and see if they feel like they serve a specific purpose—the purpose you need them to serve. Most likely your answers will lead to even more questions, unique to your app.

And now it's time to return to the goal of this chapter—the positioning statement. What is the one sentence that encapsulates all these core ideas into a call to action that makes it impossible for a potential customer not to fall in love with you immediately?

My product is _____. It does _____ in a way no other app can by _____.

Fill in the blanks, then rewrite this statement in your own words. Send it to everyone you know. Send it to your friends, your mother. Send it to nontechnical people who would be potential customers in the App Store. Send it to fellow developers.

Does the message resonate? Do these different groups of people quickly understand what you've built and why they should choose it over competitors?

Continue to refine this statement until you've found your One True Positioning Statement and *voilà!*

Congratulations!

You're one step closer to becoming an expert marketer.

But wait . . . there's more . . .

Poking Holes

The best advice I can give to anyone positioning a product is to play devil's advocate with yourself.

The second-best advice I can give you is that sometimes you are not the best judge of your own marketing work. It's incredibly difficult to be objective with yourself when you've spent so much time and energy coming up with ideas.

Find someone you trust who can be brutally honest with you—someone who will be openly critical. Imagine if the things this person says were said to you for the first time in a public setting. Chances are it's not the reaction you would want from your product launch, and this is a great way to prepare for a potential backlash from your positioning concepts.

Talk to everyone who will listen. Don't get bogged down by nondisclosure agreements and contracts and all of that. Build the app first, and then show it to everyone. If you have confidence in your product, you will be able to do this without worry. Yes, there are always people who will copy ideas and replicate months of hard work, but consumers can tell the difference between something made with love and something made to make money.

For inspiration, look at what others have done in related industries for inspiration as well. Watch how your favorite apps have become successful, and be a student of the subtle changes and revisions made to them along the way.

"It's important to learn from other apps' successes and mistakes," Acceleroto's Bryan Duke reminds us. "Don't waste someone else's joy or pain by not learning from it."[17]

Luckily—and unfortunately as well—this industry isn't mature enough to have its own set of measurements associated with success, so we need to derive other ways and techniques of determining success. The iPhone platform is a very forgiving first foray into positioning and merchandising because, given its digital nature, every action and decision you as a marketer make is measured and accounted for. This is great for you because you have instant and real-time feedback as to whether or not your ideas are working.

Don't let your ego get in the way. If the feedback isn't what you want it to be, examine what you've done to cause that and remedy it before your app is in the market. Making changes as you're building enables you to stay on track. Be honest with what you're building and how you're communicating that to the market, and your audience will respond to it.

Thinking about this *after* the launch is a recipe for disaster.

3

The Actual "Marketing" Part

Marketing Is Your Frenemy

As far as I'm concerned, marketing is the single most important piece of the product pie chart. Now, most of the people reading this book are developers who live and die by the code they write, and they may not want to hear this, or even agree with it conceptually.

Think about it, though: what good is a product if no one knows about it?

And yet, even for those who accept this idea as true, the notion of marketing as a component of the development process is something they may find alien—even appalling. Many consider "marketing" as a necessary evil, at best. At worst, marketing will be considered the enemy.

In my time as the head of marketing for Medialets, an advertising and analytics platform for mobile apps, I typically referred to myself simply as cofounder because being introduced as a marketer immediately caused me to be brushed off by the various CEOs and other decision-makers I would encounter. Many people don't like or respect marketers, yet they don't know how to market their products, either.

What's the solution?

To empower developers to understand marketing concepts. And then perhaps they'll have a greater appreciation for what a marketer brings to the planning process for a new product, and better understand how their skill set complements the rest of the team.

Does this mean you need to bring on a full-time marketer?

No.

It isn't always appropriate for an organization building iPhone and/or iPad apps at this stage in the market. A lot of the bestselling apps in the App Store were marketed by solo developers who built great products and believed in them enough to make them succeed.

That said, if you're planning on becoming a powerhouse, it would behoove you to put someone in place whose primary role is ensuring that the principles of the brand are communicated properly, and that they evolve as the products and the market do. If you don't have the resources to hire added staff, you might task someone on your existing team to be responsible for it.

Regardless of how you do it, being consistent in the marketing initiatives that you put in place will be critical to maintaining the brand that you are building.

Fundamental Elements

While there's no set roadmap for how to market your app, there are many core components that must be in place in order to build a successful marketing program. These ideas will be fleshed out in the marketing plan we will create later in this chapter, and will become more sophisticated as you revisit and refine your plan. At the core of your marketing, you must:

- Believe in your product
- Price your product appropriately

- Plan to be in it for the long haul
- Solicit feedback
- Establish and follow timelines
- Understand your competitors
- Advertise, if you wish
- Execute, execute, execute

Ultimately, it's not *just* about what you've built or who you know—it's about how you sell. Putting together the right marketing plan and materials, and having them in place *before* launching your application, will mean the difference between the presence of a polished, deliberate brand in the App Store and a disjointed and confusing message sent to the customers you wish to attract.

Old Dogs, New Tricks!

You don't have to be developing an entirely new product in order to capture the energy of the App Store platform and use it to sell your products. Even companies with existing apps can use the iPhone and iPad to refresh their business. Existing games, for example, benefit from the myriad reasons that consumers love to use their Apple devices. For example PopCap Games, based in Seattle, Washington, established themselves by being one of the most successful independent game developers on the Mac, well before the smart phone revolution, but it was the iPhone that supercharged their brand and brought their games to a new audience of passionate fans.

"We make games for everyone to enjoy," John Vechey, CEO of PopCap says.

We strive to make all of our games appeal to the broadest possible audience by ensuring they are simple and approachable. Our product positioning comes first from the games, and then from the audience. Our most popular game, *Bejeweled,* appeals most to a thirty-five-plus-year-old female demographic which is obviously rare in computer gaming. *Bejeweled* is ten years old [in 2010] and many games have released that are very similar. Fortunately we always focus on quality, and that's won out every time.

I think the iPhone is a great platform, and I like how as time goes on, quality on the iPhone is being the biggest factor for long-lasting sales.[1]

Even members of the media—who you need to have on your side if you're looking to scale your marketing initiatives—agree that building a great game is step one in marketing your application. *Wired.com*'s Brian X. Chen is among the outspoken proponents of this approach:

A lot of developers complain about how cluttered the App Store is with apps, and how difficult it is to stay in the spotlight, but I find it heartening that the apps that stay in the top 100 tend to be very intelligently coded and well designed. Long story short, the number-one thing you need to be successful in the App Store is an intrinsically interesting idea and the brains to code it.

There are a couple of different characteristics in highly successful apps. Some tend to have a lot of replay value—e.g., addictive games or games with social elements such as leaderboards. Others introduce useful functions for everyday life—e.g., *Evernote* for cloud-based notetaking. A few are novelty applications that generate short-term, viral attention. Games appear to be the most successful in terms of money making and mainstream appeal. Who doesn't enjoy gaming?[2]

The most coveted form of iPhone app marketing—garnering attention from Apple—also begins with building a great app, as Igor Pusenjak of Lima Sky, developers of the popular games *Doodle Jump* and *AniMatch,* explains:

It really helps to have a great app. Contrary to the popular belief, I think that Apple does go through great lengths to find and feature interesting and unique apps. Of course, you will have a much better chance to be "found" if you have a contact of someone in Apple and write them a nice email explaining what makes your app unique and why should it be considered to be featured.[3]

Mark Jardine of Tapbots has seen measureable marketing results that stem from his company's confidence in the products they've built:

> We haven't quite figured it out yet. but that doesn't really bother us. Our apps sell fairly consistently over a long period of time and we get nice bumps when Apple decides to promote us. We absolutely love what we are doing and are happy as long as we can keep creating apps for a living.[4]

Parallel Paths

It's hard for others to promote your application if even you don't know how to explain its merits. That's why you've learned how to *position.*

It's equally hard to create a convincing marketing program if you can't vocalize your app's quality, uniqueness, and usefulness. This is why you've learned how to create a *positioning statement.*

It's *irrevocably* hard to sell applications if you don't believe in your product. You must build a great app that you are not just content, but *thrilled* to put your name on. It doesn't need to be perfect, but you have to believe in your product's idea. You are the foremost one who can instill confidence in others.

"A great app can be the window of a company's soul," Shazam's Kathleen McMahon extols.

Users can sense authenticity. They can sense the level of expertise and care put into an app and intent. In turn, a great app enables a developer or a company to see and reach users in ways that were impossible before.

The connection is extremely direct.[5]

As you develop your app, you are surrounded by the creative energy that will make it a killer. While you are engulfed in that energy, capture it, identify it, and record it. Your audience will be excited by the very things that thrill you about your app. What drives you to create will drive them to buy your product. So by developing your marketing ideas in a path that runs parallel to your technical development, you'll avoid missing some of the most potent material you could use when your app goes to market.

"If you can market your app to reflect the *culture* of your app— your company, your mission, whatever it is you are trying to achieve—and do it authentically, you have the wheels in motion. If it's simply about making money, you are missing the point," explains App Cubby's David Barnard, developer of the popular gasoline mileage and vehicle maintenance app *Gas Cubby.*

For me, the marketing process starts when I'm brainstorming app ideas. If the app won't make a splash or have an interesting marketing angle, it's really tough to justify putting in any time and/or money to build it.

This might sound a bit pretentious, but *Gas Cubby* is an awesome app! It's not perfect, there's so much more I'd love to do, but it's a really great app and something I'm incredibly proud of. When I talk to the press or work on other marketing, I'm not blowing smoke or trying to swindle App Store shoppers, I'm talking about an app I genuinely think is worth learning about and ultimately, worth buying.

Don't underestimate the incredible psychological impact of selling something you deeply care about and truly believe in.[6]

Brands with Legs—*Nice-looking* Legs

Developers like Barnard showed ambition not just because they attempted to build applications in the early days of the App Store, although that is certainly a praiseworthy accomplishment. Even before they knew how the market would take shape, they began their ventures with the intention of creating *lasting* brands, with great apps as the foundation and root of their ambitions.

"When the initial ideas for *App Cubby* started to take shape back in March of 2008, I decided that I didn't want to create a few quick apps and just see how things played out," Barnard recalls. "My goal was to lay the foundation for a brand that would become a trusted name in the App Store."[7]

Brand perception is an important part of the marketing process, starting with basics such as logo design that many brush over as unimportant or even petty. Customers begin forming an opinion about your application from the first moment they see your app's icon, so paying attention to each and every component of the branding process is paramount when building a great app.

"With such a lofty goal, I knew that visual branding was going to play a very important role," Barnard continues. "My first task was to find an artist to bring this plan to fruition. Well, being the insanely compulsive person I am, I ended up working with three freelance artists and spending over $4,000 on icons and other artwork."[8]

For the average entry-level iPhone developer it's difficult to spend much time and money on art when there's no guarantee that an app will make any money at all, but it's especially tough to get much attention, especially from Apple, if an app's icon and other artwork are subpar.

Keep in mind that you don't have to reinvent the wheel when coming up with new app ideas. The question you ought to ask yourself is, Can I build the best app possible, and does it have a unique enough angle to make it marketable?

Tapbots, the maker of *Weightbot* and *Pastebot,* has become well known in the app ecosystem for creating elegant, attractive, and well-built applications based on basic functionality. Its founders held firmly to their belief that design was critical to attracting customers and retaining them, and the result has been success in the App Store.

"It's no secret that our apps stand out from the crowd. But being different is just part of the puzzle. You need to deliver a great experience, as well," Mark Jardine, cofounder of Tapbots, explains.

> People say our apps aren't innovative in the sense that they don't solve a new problem. Just because there are thirty unit conversion apps on the store, doesn't mean another one can't be successful.
>
> The great thing about the iPhone app market is apps are cheap. People aren't heavily invested in a single application. If they paid ninety-nine cents for a unit converter, they'll have no problem buying another one if it's better. So when we decide to do an application, it doesn't matter how many of them are on the store. In fact, nine times out of ten, there are probably already at least five to ten apps based on your groundbreaking idea.
>
> Our apps can be described simply as utility robots that are easy to use, focused, and lots of fun. When we were brainstorming ideas for our first app, *Weightbot,* a weight tracker, the movie *Wall-E* came to mind—I'm a huge Pixar fan. Specifically, the concept of simple robots that perform just one task. They all had a unique design, yet felt part of the same family of BNL [the faux company in the movie]. Eve became a source of inspiration for the design of *Weightbot* and everything just fell into place from there. We felt we had a concept that would allow us to build strong brand recognition and allow us enough creative freedom to make fun, memorable apps.
>
> We study the best three to four of a particular type of app and ask ourselves, "Could we do it better?" We ask ourselves very simple questions when deciding on an app to develop.

1. Can we sell it to the majority?
2. Will we enjoy building it?
3. Will we use it ourselves?
4. Can we do better than the current competition?

If the answer is yes to all four, then there's a good chance we might build it eventually.[9]

John Casasanta of tap tap tap experienced similar success in the App Store by building a better mousetrap:

> It's important to realize that an idea for an app doesn't always have to be some new, groundbreaking concept. Take our unit converter app *Convert,* for instance. By the time we launched it, there were literally dozens of other unit converters in the App Store. But we tried hard to create the one with the best UI and market it very aggressively. I feel like we succeeded as it ranked as high as number two and has sold hundreds of thousands of copies in a short time.[10]

Novelty of idea is certainly a competitive advantage that can kick-start the marketing process for a new app developer.

A Cost-Free Army of Consultants

"My first iPhone app, *Air Hockey,* was the result of brainstorming and user response," Bryan Duke, founder of Acceleroto, recalls. *Air Hockey* has been selected as a staff pick in the store, ranked as high as number one in the paid application category, and was the number two overall app in early September 2008.

> When the SDK was first announced, I thought for several weeks about what would make a great app for the iPhone. The device's features—such as network connectivity, multitouch, and speed—were

major drivers in the things I considered. I decided that a fast-paced and responsive game that took advantage of multitouch would be the way to go. *Air Hockey*'s first version grew from that seed.

Step one was to make the best product I knew how. As early as possible, I start marketing it. In the very early stages of development, I come up with a code name for the app and start talking about the code name on Twitter and forums. I want to move this. Where should it go?

My second game, *Occurro!* was known as *Project Driftwood* in the early days. People didn't know what it was, but talking about it certainly didn't hurt. As soon as the art is semi-finalized, I release icons or screen shots. As soon as gameplay is close, I release a trailer. Once it's submitted to Apple, I do everything possible—within budget— to make sure Apple and review sites take note.[11]

Be willing to iterate on your idea, and be receptive to early customer response.

When reaching out to your customer base, think about what you're asking them to do. Much like the sales meeting scenario I explained earlier, you don't want to blast an email to all of your customers without giving them a specific task to accomplish or asking for something in particular. While your customers and friends want to help you, they likely don't have the time and energy to determine what it is you need help with.

Make it easy for your customers to assist you in this process and you will yield a much higher response rate from your request.

There are no guidelines telling you how much should you reveal and how much should you keep under wraps. If you have some very proprietary technology or you have a good reason to keep your app's functionality confidential, you may want to ask your reviewers to sign a nondisclosure agreement (NDA). Bear in mind, though, that this may be a turnoff to a lot of people who don't want to sign a legally binding contract just to review your app.

If you are in the process of selling your app or need some trusted individuals to help with due diligence, you may want to risk turning some people off to get the right feedback, yet preserve your property.

But if your app isn't top secret, your customer base or beta tester group should be able to help you think of components or facets for your app that you may have overlooked or underappreciated. Giving your testers the opportunity to be very critical will help you deliver the best app possible to the market.

When soliciting feedback, you may want to break up your list into discrete requests: one group gives feedback on design, another on functionality, yet another on usability, and so on. This will keep your group from feeling overwhelmed with too many questions all at once and will make the insights and feedback easier to incorporate. As Acceleroto's Bryan Duke says:

> At launch, *Air Hockey* was a two-player-only game where one person played from one end of the screen and another person played from the other. The two-player mode worked great, but the real transformation that made the game a winner was adding killer one-player modes.
>
> How'd I know that would work?
>
> I listened to my customers. The feedback from my first version of *Air Hockey* all went something like "good, but I really need something I can play when I'm standing in line at the store." I designed the computer opponent's AI by watching people play the real version of air hockey. The first version of the AI was so good that none of my beta testers could score against it. After lots of tweaks with the test team, I came up with easy, medium, and hard AI difficulties that made sense. People loved them and the new update shot *Air Hockey* to the top of the charts.[12]

Duke also has advice for the developer who is trying to position an app:

Polish, service, and awesomeness are critical to making a successful iPhone app. An app that looks good on first impression will probably generate more sales than one that's ugly. Spend money on professional graphics. Do interface testing. Get as much feedback as you can before and after you launch. Once you start selling, provide the best customer support you can. If one customer reports a problem, run it to the ground. There are probably many others with the same problem that won't contact you. You won't get anywhere unless you have a good product to begin with. It's also important to learn from other apps' successes and mistakes. Don't waste someone else's joy or pain by not learning from it.[13]

Timing Is Critical

Matt Martel, founder of Mundue LLC, has been one of the fortunate to build a game, *reMovem*, that soared to the number-one ranking in the free category in 2008. To date, *reMovem* free has achieved more than 5 million downloads. Martel says:

> For me, timing was everything, my primary expertise is in development, with graphics, marketing, accounting, etcetera, taking a backseat. What I did have was a passion for Mac and subsequently the iPhone platform. I think that the most significant move I made strategically was to jump on the iPhone bandwagon early with a fun, simple, addicting game.[14]

Martel had noticed a consistent surge around the Christmas holiday when consumers were spending time in the App Store and spending their newly acquired money and gift cards:

> With *reMovem* free, it was obviously a success from the beginning. It took quite a bit longer for the paid version to catch on, but it has

generated far fewer overall downloads. We used a variety of techniques to promote the paid version, and these finally started to deliver in January of '09. This of course coincided with the Christmas surge and the end-of-year top number ten posting by Apple.[15]

Timing your launch around events that lead users to need your application is a surefire way to create demand for your app. This was famously the case for the geolocation and social networking application *foursquare.*

Naveen Selvadurai recalls:

My cofounder, Dennis [Crowley] and I had been experimenting in the space for a little while before we came together and brought our ideas to form *foursquare.* We initially seeded the product to a few of our closest friends to see how they'd use it. When [the influential technology conference] South By Southwest came around, we just knew it was going to be a great place to launch the app, so we worked hard to get to that deadline and launched it there. The app went live in the App Store literally hours before SXSW Interactive officially started.[16]

Marketing an iPhone app is like climbing a hill—a really steep hill. The climb up is very difficult, but once you've hit the top it's smooth sailing—until you're at the bottom again. Marketing success in the App Store typically happens in spikes. Customers purchase certain types of applications at certain times of the year: recipe apps around Thanksgiving, study guides in autumn when students go back to school . . . the list is endless.

Communicate the reasons your app is a must-have and use timing to your advantage. You want to be front and center with the best applications possible when your target audience is looking for an app like yours.

Stay relevant. Think like your customers and they'll reward you by choosing your app over the other 100,000 they could be downloading.

Again, Know Your Competition

There is a secret weapon in determining how to market in an environment with multiple competitors: it's called a SWOT analysis. SWOT stands for:

Strengths
Weaknesses
Opportunities
Threats

The SWOT is one of those lessons I learned while studying marketing in college. It seemed so annoying at the time, but it has become invaluable to me as a business professional. I haven't subjected you to much Marketing 101 material, but this lesson will be a huge asset to your marketing arsenal. If you execute it honestly and completely, you will uncover many opportunities that could make or break your app's long-term success in this market.

To give you a little more background about the SWOT and how it is used, take a look at Table 3.1.

Table 3.1

Strengths	Weaknesses
Opportunities	Threats

As you can see, the strengths and opportunities are aligned on the left side and the weaknesses and threats on the right. Even though the four quadrants represent completely unique elements, when determining competitive positioning, strengths often offer opportunities and weaknesses are subject to threats.

The SWOT analysis is primarily used for strategic planning because these high-level concepts lend themselves to coming up with tactics that will enable you to counteract the threats you identify. The SWOT typically encompasses both internal and external threats, so be sure to give a complete and honest evaluation when filling out the matrix.

The SWOT technique has been helping companies with their competitive strategies since the 1960s, when business consultant Albert Humphrey presented them at a convention at Stanford University. I can assure you that the lessons from his technique will be invaluable in setting your marketing program.

Guidelines for Each Quadrant

- Strengths: qualities of the application that are defensible or powerful in marketing it
- Weaknesses: aspects of the app that are inadequate or weak compared to other apps
- Opportunities: external elements helpful to accomplishing sales, buzz, etc.
- Threats: external factors that could be detrimental to achieving your ultimate goals

Table 3.2 on the following page shows an example of the matrix filled out for a theoretical app, a *DJing* application for the iPad.

Now fill this matrix out for your app, and the apps of your top three competitors. This will show how well you stack up, but you don't need to stop there. You can continue for each additional competitor or potential competitor that you believe could be a threat to your ability to gain users.

Aim for at least four to five bullet points for each quadrant of the matrix shown in Table 3.3.

Table 3.2

Strengths	Weaknesses
Novel concept, new functionality, enjoyable to use, instant gratification by the user, well-designed app that is more robust than competitors in the market	Limited functionality, restricted by Apple's SDK policies regarding importing music from the iTunes app, high price point, small team so updates are infrequent
Opportunities	Threats
Visibility in the market thanks to the customers who use it in live performance, partner with well-known DJs to generate buzz, lengthy engagement by users, possibly a candidate for iAd	Lower-priced competitors may steal market share, space is beginning to get crowded, brand is not yet established in the market, app can occasionally crash when user attempts complicated scratches

Table 3.3

Your App	
Strengths	Weaknesses
Opportunities	Threats

Competitor No. 1

Strengths	Weaknesses

Opportunities	Threats

Competitor No. 2

Strengths	Weaknesses

Opportunities	Threats

Competitor No. 3

Strengths	Weaknesses
Opportunities	Threats

Applying Polish

Polish is the secret weapon in a great marketing initiative.

In some ways, this is inherently counterintuitive to the speed at which technology moves. There is a delicate balance between fast and good. However, you need both in order to succeed in this market. It's why Apple itself has dominated the technology world. Everything Apple does oozes *Apple*. The typefaces, the packaging, the minimalism, the Web copy, everything has a brand identity that shines through and creates loyalty. And at the core, the products are good. They merit the branding that's been put around them.

So let's break down everything I just expressed as Apple's great strengths and find a way to apply them to your business and your iPhone apps.

Brand Identity

Ask a designer what this means and he or she will most likely tell you it's a logo. Yes, a logo does express what the identity of a brand is, but it's also the icing on the cake of a brand's presentation to the world. There are a lot of factors that influence the design of a brand's logo, and in the marketing world this is called establishing brand identity. It is the set of characteristics and attributes that come to mind when consumers think about a brand.

When setting out to create a brand identity, think long term—consider where you will be a year from now. Build around the *potential* of your brand rather than just the immediate needs. You can always refine your logo, but the principles that guide your brand in the App Store should be established from the outset.

There are many facets that contribute to polish in the App Store. Company name, product name, length of name, number of syllables, logo color, logo font: they all play a part in the psychology of trust and a customer's willingness to try your product. What does your app stand for? Is this something that a user can feel good about or relate to?

Think back to the Airwalk example Malcolm Gladwell described in *The Tipping Point*. There was an exchange that took place between Airwalk and consumers. Airwalks were designed to be cool, and wearers of Airwalks were cool by association. In marketing, a lot of attention is paid to ensuring that the needs of the customer are met when related to brand identity.

When designing an iPhone app, you have an obligation to those who will download it: to live up to what you've told them the app will be.

Brand Loyalty

If your brand identity and position stick with consumers, something amazing happens.

Users begin to trust your products.

They will download your apps sight unseen because you have demonstrated consistency and value to them, whether that's entertainment value, economic value, utility, or any other reason customers love your app more than anyone else's.

This is called brand loyalty.

When customers are loyal to your brand, they are willing to promote your app to others, unprovoked. A third party's endorsement of a product is more powerful than any first-party marketing can be. The goal of marketing your apps is to reach the broadest audience possible and to convince the market that your app is worth having. Amassing loyal customers is *critical* to accomplishing this.

Be careful, though, to live up to expectations. If you are known to your constituency for quality and then release an app that was rushed, your core customers may feel disappointed or even betrayed by your brand. Think of this like the relationship you have with your favorite band. If you always count on it to deliver rock anthems, and their highly anticipated new album consists of experimental indie music, you may feel let down.

As you build your applications, be sure to adhere to the brand guidelines you have put in place, because they provide a blueprint you will use to build your business. You can refine and polish, but don't forget this road map as you evolve and mature in the App Store ecosystem.

Employing Pricing Strategies

One of the key facets of marketing is pricing strategy, yet it is seldom discussed in marketing texts. Among software developers, price points are typically decided arbitrarily; they rarely represent more than a number chosen by gut reaction. It's always a good idea to select a price point based on the value your app brings to users, but there's much more to it than that.

And in the App Store, $0.99 is not the way to stand out.

As we discussed in the beginning of the book, the App Store has undergone a lot of changes since its early days. Developers tried every trick in the book—regardless of the means—to achieve the sales numbers they felt their app merited. Those developing on the iPhone platform continue to pay the price for these machinations, because we are now experiencing the phenomenon known as "price compression."

It breaks down like this.

Developers wanted to sell their apps, so instead of increasing their marketing activities to drive awareness and sales, they decreased their prices. All of the sudden there was a race to the $0.99 price point, because it was easier to follow along with the trend rather than put in the time and energy to do the job right.

Price compression and competition from free apps are the reasons developers tell themselves they have been brutally *forced* to price their apps at $0.99. Some developers have tried to justify the low price by incorporating advertising into their apps, in an effort to generate a secondary revenue stream to make up for the money they're *not* making by selling the fruits of their labors.

But the fact is that most free apps aren't really ad-sustainable. And in many segments of the store the faux threat of competition from lower-priced apps prevents great apps from reaching their full potential.

Remember, your price may tell the customer how much you *think* your app is worth, and $0.99 doesn't say much for your confidence in your product. The assumption is that you get what you pay for.

Certainly there are many consumers who will look for the lowest price option for a product, but there are far more opportunities to turn price point into a sales and marketing strategy, particularly if all other components of the marketing program are put into place.

Consumers are willing to pay reasonable prices.

Remember the law of diminishing marginal utility: a thing is only worth as much as someone is willing to pay for it at the time of purchase. So if consumer number one is in a bind and needs the *best* camera application on the iPhone, and there's an option between a $0.99 app and a $9.99 app, that user is most likely going to equate price point with quality. That is a ten-times-higher difference in revenue to the developer of the higher-priced application.

That's very significant.

As much as the customer may like the product that's one-tenth the cost, she may also see it as one-tenth the value, and perhaps even one-tenth the quality. Even if it's just as good as the higher-priced alternative!

Additionally—and far more important—it's nearly impossible to move up-market if you're the cut-rate product. Would you go to Walmart to buy a name-brand luxury item? I'm going to guess not. It's not even that Walmart *couldn't* sell Chanel handbags if it wanted to—it's that the consumers who buy Chanel handbags wouldn't likely be looking for them at Walmart.

Walmart has built its brand around being the economical choice because it buys in bulk. Items bought in bulk are often of lower quality, and the result is lower prices. So as a consumer, if money is no object, you wouldn't likely think first of Walmart when purchasing luxury goods. Indeed, Walmart understands its customers well enough to know why its customers shop there.

There are lots of lessons to be learned from this example. Apply them to your own situation.

What about "free"?

There will always be free applications in the App Store, so if you're looking to charge for your application, don't view this price point as competitive—a common mistake developers make when determining their pricing. It's an entirely different approach to selling. If you are releasing a free application, make that point front and center in your marketing messages.

Make pricing work for you. Consumers are willing to accept your rationale for picking your price point. Don't choose the number arbitrarily. Build good software and charge for it appropriately.

Take back your price point—but do it from the beginning.

As the market matures, developers have become more savvy about their pricing strategies, PopCap's CEO John Vechey explains:

> Our most popular game, *Bejeweled,* launched with the App Store. We figured it would be a success, but a year and a half later it's still in the top 10, and has never ventured out of the top 25. We've since launched two other games, *Bookworm* and *Peggle.* Interestingly enough, with *Peggle,* we've experimented a lot with limited-time sales and various price points so much that a few websites have coined a term, "peggling"—that is, lower the price of a game to get it on the top selling, then raise the price to take advantage of its high place on the charts.[17]

Mundue LLC's Matt Martel tried a different approach:

> With *reMovem* my biggest success resulted from the timing of the release of the free version and my decision to use a hybrid model of free and paid apps. I stated very early on that *reMovem* free would remain free forever and I've honored that. This was at a time when developers were flipping apps to game the system, so although keeping a free app free may not appear to be such a difficult decision in retrospect, it was not the obvious or even typical decision at that time.
>
> I have no doubt that I would have increased revenue had I flipped, but I decided to do what felt right for me. I did add a nag to the free version to promote the sales of the other, and I put ads in the free version. I believe that there are a certain number of people who will not pay for an app, and if you want name recognition you can't afford to ignore them.
>
> That strategy has worked well.[18]

To Advertise or Not to Advertise

Honestly, if budget weren't an issue for indie and first-time app developers, this section could be named "Where to Spend Your Advertising Dollars." But given the nature and nascence of the App Store and the fact that most people reading this book won't be sitting atop million-dollar marketing budget allocations, I'm going to assume that determining whether or not to spend precious dollars on ads is a wise move.

Ideally, when you've built a well-positioned application that has gone through all the motions of setting up a winning place in the App Store, paying for ads won't be necessary to build the buzz necessary to drive sales.

Perhaps.

For example, *RunKeeper*—which in December 2009 was named among the top 10 iPhone apps by *Time* magazine, best of 2009 by Lifehacker, *Wired,* and CNET, and best location-based mobile app by Mashable—achieved this level of success with no advertising. *RunKeeper* is an application that uses the iPhone's built-in GPS to enable runners, cyclists, and other fitness enthusiasts to use the iPhone to track their outdoor fitness activities, including time, distance, pace, calories burned, and path traveled on a map. It integrates with a Web-based online community where users can store all their historical activities, share them with friends, and post them to social sites like Facebook and Twitter.

"Since we started out with almost no marketing budget, advertising was not an option," *RunKeeper*'s Jason Jacobs recalls.

> Instead, we focused on building a great product that users like, making it easy for them to spread the word by auto-posting their activities to Twitter and/or Facebook, and getting the media to write about us in order to build awareness. We also did some marketing campaigns, the most notable being when I ran the Boston Marathon

dressed as a giant iPhone with the *RunKeeper* app on the screen, and launched a series of viral videos leading up to the race to build awareness. This campaign ended up being covered by dozens of major media publications, including the *New York Times, Boston Globe, AdWeek, PR Week,* and many others.

While we do believe advertising can be effective and should not be discounted, what started as our only option due to limited funds ended up being more effective than if we had spent money on advertising in the first place. Now that we have a bigger marketing budget, it will be interesting to see whether we start using it on more traditional methods like advertising, or if we stick to our nontraditional core knitting. I guess a combo of both is possible, too, although there is something alluring about powering through without doing what everyone used to think needs to be done and spending money on ads.[19]

tap tap tap's John Casasanta has evolved his company's advertising strategy as the App Store has matured. He notes that as difficult as it is to become one of the top-selling apps in the store today, the cost of advertising to a large enough audience would be prohibitive:

As far as advertising goes, we've basically abandoned just about all advertising. It simply doesn't work, except in a few rare instances. For people who've followed along with our company blog since the early days, this may come as a bit of a surprise since we've documented our early strategy of buying up as much ad inventory at the lowest cost possible to blast our apps up the ranks.

Once the app was charting, the exposure and added sales from being in the top charts would be more than enough to pay for the ads. In the early days this would work, since the barrier to entry into the top 100 was much lower than it is now. But these days, it's essentially impossible to make this method pay off.[20]

Other app developers such as *reMovem*'s Matt Martel do see the limited value in spending initial budget on ads in order to break through all of the noise of the store:

> Originally it was just a website and an appeal for reviews. Later we tried press releases—to mixed success—and advertisements in print and online as well as in-app ads. I feel that ads are ineffective, but do have some merit as far as keeping the app names visible in users' faces.[21]

Some developers may not be able to justify spending their money on buying ad space, but what about alternative forms of advertising?

Birdhouse, an application developed by Adam Lisagor and Cameron Hunt, received a lot of media attention around the independently created commercial they shot for their application and released online. Their company, Sandwich Dynamics, was thrust from obscurity to overnight fame among the app development community, who scrambled to replicate their methodology around promoting *Birdhouse.*

Birdhouse's approach was novel and noteworthy because its developers were among the first of their kind to treat their app as a real product.

"A well-made video demonstrating the app's functions and uses is vitally important," Sandwich Dynamic's headmaster Adam Lisagor explains.

> One reason the iPhone commercials are so successful is because we, the audience, get to see the device and its software operate as though it is in our own hands, from our own perspective. Each commercial has a self-contained narrative: you need this, you have this, you do this, and you end up better off than you were. If you can craft a story through the medium of video that tells the user why he or she needs your app, how he or she will use it, and why it will make life better, then you are that much closer to selling your app.

And if you can make it entertaining like the *Birdhouse* video, which is a skill and an industry in itself, you're miles ahead of the rest of the apps out there. We got a massive amount of feedback which explicitly told us, "I don't know if I'll use *Birdhouse,* but I bought it because the video was funny." Can't get much better pudding proof than that.

We've only done the tiniest bit of traditional advertising. And that was generously donated by friends with high-profile blogs and ad networks. Well-placed ads have given *Birdhouse* a nice boost, no doubt, but that is short-lived and the best marketing will always be positive feedback from happy users, which is generally free of charge.

When people like to use something, they enjoy telling people about it. The nature of the current open and easy self-publishing infrastructure on today's Internet makes it practical and rewarding for your customers to tell people about the things they like. So it all comes back around to making something for people to enjoy.[22]

Fundamentally, you can choose between promoting through earned media or paid media.

"Earned media" is any free media coverage. Blogs, radio, even social media are all considered earned media.

Anything you pay for—ad spots, sponsorships, and the like—fall into the "paid media" category. If you're really smart, you'll strike a balance between the two.

But as I said in the beginning, this isn't a chapter about where to spend your advertising dollars. I think that if you're very strategic, you can come up with a good marketing mix that includes timed PR campaigning around the launch of an app and then spend whatever you're comfortable with in order to support it with paid initiatives. I happen to be a proponent of sponsoring parties at key conferences. In my experience, that yields the greatest bang for your buck with the highest brand retention rates.

Think about what you're trying to achieve before you spend your first dollar on advertising. If you can't clearly communicate what it is you're looking for in terms of return on investment, rethink spending your money. Each initiative should be tailored toward accomplishing a strategic objective. Frivolous spending will only discourage you from working on your app's promotion for the long haul.

Money can't buy you love, baby. You have to earn that.

Know Your Audience

One of the questions in the positioning workbook section of the previous chapter referred to your audience. You may have the ability to identify them now, but how much do you *know* about them? Taking the time to truly research and understand your potential customers will give you the tools you need to approach selling to them, appropriately and efficiently.

Adam Lisagor of Sandwich Dynamics agrees:

Birdhouse is a publishing tool for Twitter, specifically, and it has always been created for and targeted to a certain demographic of Twitter users—those who enjoy the creative and self-expressive uses of Twitter. With that in mind, *Birdhouse* has always been a perfect fit in the message-spreading channels of Twitter. We appealed to our audience's need for a creative tool—a need which had never been addressed. And it was important to us to appeal to this need in a creative way.

So we did it with humor. And our idea was just different enough from everything else out there that it made people stop and think and wonder why our idea had even been created, whether they would even need it, why no one had thought of it before. And if you get your target audience to even stop and ask themselves questions, it's a good thing.[23]

PopCap Games CEO John Vechey offers his perspective:

Our internal marketing department spends a lot of time working with the internal game studio, to match what makes sense to the consumer with what the core of the game is. From a strategic point of view, Pop-Cap has Andrew Stein, formerly of AT&T, who is our director of mobile. He works with the marketing and studio departments on ensuring any tactics on the iPhone line up with our overall tactics on mobile.

This has resulted in a measurable increase in sales.[24]

It's very common, however, to believe that your audience is one group when they are actually an entirely different demographic, as was the case with Lima Sky's hit title *AniMatch*.

"Our success actually happened organically, by observing the response of the marketplace," Lima Sky's Igor Pusenjak explains.

We were initially positioning our bestselling kids' title, *AniMatch,* as a game that everyone can enjoy. This was partially out of fear that the market for kids' iPhone games was too small—which in some ways at that time it was—and partially due to the fact that all our "grown-up" friends seem to have enjoyed it a lot.

However, as we started seeing that people were buying *AniMatch* almost exclusively for their kids, we shifted the focus. While we still mention that the game can be enjoyed by everyone, we are primarily positioning it as a kids' title now.[25]

Enable a Call to Action

In sales, there is a concept known as an "ask."

The purpose of a sales presentation is to present an idea and persuade the customer to buy something, but many times salespeople forget to *ask* for it. In other words, salespeople can spend hours crafting a story and preaching it, but ultimately do not ask the customer to *do* anything. Without any actionable steps to be completed by the customer, the salesperson is participating in a one-way conversation, and this seldom leads to a sale.

As an iPhone and iPad developer, you are selling to customers. You may not be engaged in a sales meeting, per se, but you are selling just the same. If you are selling via advertising or marketing, you must present a call to action. If your app is not on the market yet, ask for an email address so you can supply updates and announcements. If you're on Twitter, ask users to follow you there. If your app is in the App Store, ask users to download it.

Even if you don't make an immediate sale, the act of engaging with the customer is essential.

Marketing and advertising your product will only be as effective as the call to action you've generated. Anytime you present information of a persuasive nature, you should provide your consumer with the opportunity to do something as a result of his or her current motivation. You cannot bank on a user remembering the name of your app, or recalling the marketing campaign in your ad.

Provide an immediate action—however large, small, simple, or complex—that will *engage* the user and will also let you measure the metrics and statistics that relate specifically to interested consumers—for example, five thousand email signups, 75 percent male users, 40 percent of your users are on Twitter, and so on.

RunKeeper's Jason Jacobs describes his approach to creating a viral environment around his application and to capturing the media buzz in a measurable and actionable way:

> Before we launched, we gave users a place to sign up to be notified when we went live, and we had gotten quite a bit of media attention. So by the time we went live, it was off to the races. We were a little, bootstrapped startup, and we brought in more than $50,000 in revenue in the first three months.[26]

This type of data capture, enabling interested users to sign up to find out when the app will be released, is an unbelievably powerful resource to have at your disposal. These are opt-in marketing opportunities, and you can use the list you build to remarket to this group every time you release an app.

And once you have a direct line to your customers, you have a better chance of inciting them to spread the word.

Adam Lisagor explains:

[*Birdhouse* senior developer] Cameron Hunt had a great idea for enabling a call to action, to preload *Birdhouse* with a prefabricated draft of a tweet which cryptically states: "This is my *Birdhouse*. There are many like it, but this one is mine." We had no idea whether people would be compelled to publish the predrafted tweet, but we knew that if they did, it would pique the interest of those followers who saw the message.

And lo! and behold, people not only began to publish the message, they began to put their own creative spin on it, and the message became a meme in and of itself. There is no better example of a message spreading through the exact perfect channels to the exact perfect audience for the exact perfect reasons. If a developer can find a similar way to compel his or her users to spread the word through pure and organic channels, it can go a long, long way toward a wider adoption of the app itself.[27]

Calls to action aren't just about sales conversions; they are also about gathering demographic and user information relating to those who are interested in your product. Be sure to provide an opportunity to capture data—in whatever form you can—about those who have expressed a genuine interest in your app. Measurements, such as the number of people on your email list or number of Twitter followers for your app's account, will be critical to launching and marketing a product.

If you can't measure growth, how can you know what's working and what's not? This data is absolutely critical to making informed decisions about your customer base.

Engagement as a Marketing Tool

Stay top-of-mind to your core audience and fans by using the tools at your disposal, such as email lists, Twitter, Facebook, meetups, and all the other digital means of making real connections with your potential customers. This is absolutely critical during both pre- and post-launch in order to establish and maintain a winning position in the market.

"One way to engage users is by continually improving the app and by nurturing a growing, thriving community of users who are as excited about interacting with each other as they are about using the app," recommends *RunKeeper*'s Jason Jacobs.

> Plugging the app into a larger system, in our case, on the Web, and making a concerted effort to continually improve around the app have been really successful for us. That way, even if the app stays the same, if the system that it plugs into keeps getting better and a user needs our app to take part in this system, the value of the app keeps increasing as well.[28]

But engagement needs to be an ongoing process—it never ends, and if it does end, your audience will likely go elsewhere.

> A big marketing strategy for us was to be very responsive to users, both in our forum on the website, but also using Twitter to engage with users who were talking about us on the social Web" [says Jacobs]. Users really appreciated the accessibility and the human face

this put on our business, and has been a major differentiator for us versus our competition."[29]

Leverage social media to build buzz and don't be shy about engaging with your customer base on these platforms. Sandwich Dynamics, whose primary product is a Twitter app, happens to have gotten this strategy right by using the platform to its advantage.

"*Birdhouse* has a Twitter account for updating users and followers on upcoming releases and notes about current versions," says Adam Lisagor.

> We try to maintain a certain amount of character in our Twitter stream, with the spirit of creativity and humor intact. We have a separate Twitter account that is only for responding to comments and questions we receive on Twitter. That way, our main news Twitter doesn't get cluttered with the detritus of conversation. And as a result, even before our launch, we'd generated enough interest with our mildly entertaining Twitter feed to amass hundreds of followers, curious about what it is we were making. Stay connected to your users. They appreciate being thought of and—as we've learned from Apple and other companies—hate being ignored.[30]

The Apple Grail

All the marketing in the world won't match the impact Apple can have on your product.

Typically, in a retail environment, store owners are able to select the products they wish to promote. The process for being promoted within the App Store, however, is more akin to trying to land major publicity. Companies and individuals don't know when they'll be selected to be interviewed for a piece in the *New York Times,* but you better believe they'll be ready at a moment's notice when called upon with such an opportunity.

Similarly, manufacturers move heaven and earth to secure a place in Walmart or a boutique in Macy's. A prominent place in the iTunes store is such a holy grail.

You don't know when Apple is going to call, and in the App Store culture, it's even more nebulous—because the industry and platform are so new and Apple gets to set the ground rules for how they showcase apps. Even two years into this ecosystem, the process remains a mystery, but a few case studies have emerged for developers to follow.

RunKeeper's success has been measurably impacted by being chosen by Apple for its advertising campaigns.

"Our big break was when Apple started featuring us in full page newspaper ads in the *Wall Street Journal,* the *New York Times, USAToday,* [and other publications]," Jason Jacobs notes.

> We had no knowledge they were going to pick us, but in hindsight, it must have been because we had a large, growing community of users, there was lots of buzz and media attention around us, and our application was being reviewed very well by users.
>
> My guess is Apple was looking for applications to feature that would cater to a large group of potential iPhone owners, showcase unique features of the iPhone, and help Apple sell more iPhones by reflecting well on the device.
>
> The best way to get featured by Apple—from what I can see—is to not focus on getting Apple's attention at all. Rather, focus on building a great app that is solid, design up to Apple design standards, that people like, and that gets a large community of happy users. The more PR and awareness you are able to generate outside of the Apple ecosystem, the more likely Apple will swoop in and feature you within their ecosystem.
>
> Conversely, if you approach them to feature you without going and doing all of the things I mentioned above, your odds of getting

successfully featured drop down quite a bit. I can't say for sure that this is true, but this has been our philosophy and it has worked well for us. Of course, we are still holding out for the TV commercial, so we still have some work left to do![31]

While many detest Apple's closed environment and are quick to criticize Apple's methods and practices, these same people crave the validation of being one of the "chosen ones."

"Apple. Apple. Apple," David Barnard sighs. "After *Health Cubby*'s poor launch and the ensuing financial tail spin, Apple selected *Gas Cubby* as its "App Store Pick of the Week." Graph 3.1 speaks for itself . . .[32]

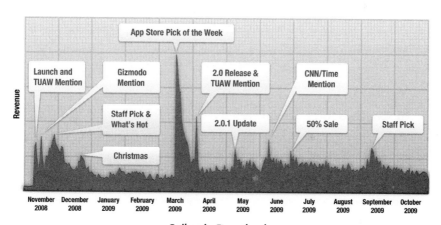

Spikes in Downloads

An iPhone developer can't count on Apple featuring their app, unless that developer is EA, Gameloft, or one of a handful of high profile developers [Barnard continues], but exposure within the App Store is by far the best kind of exposure an app can get. Given that, I'm very conscious of spending time on features and doing things that are likely to get Apple's attention, such as implementing their latest and greatest technologies.

So, in a lot of ways I market to Apple as much as I market to App Store shoppers. If Apple likes your app, there's a pretty darn good chance customers will as well, and if Apple features your app, there's a much better chance those customers will ever find your app.[33]

Jenna Wortham, a technology reporter at the *New York Times* who covers start-ups and the mobile industry, echoes what others have said:

As the App Store continues to evolve from a kitschy catalog of novelty applications into a platform that is rapidly transforming mobile computing, more and more developers—from the indie garage outfits to venture-backed startups and large companies—will clamor to write software for the iPhone, iPod Touch, and any other Apple devices that can run the bite-sized programs.

Which only means the competition is going to get stiffer.

And I think that what will help differentiate applications in the longer run will be the same features as we found in the ones that had such booming success in the earlier days of the App Store. Those that find some creative new way to make use of the device's features or have genuine functionality beyond just a gimmicky app that translates whatever you're saying into the language of the Na'vi or whatever. To be sure, there is still room for those apps to have success, but I think the game will change somewhat in terms of what garners serious attention from Apple and the media.[34]

"Getting *Air Hockey* into the top 100 games chart was the big hurdle," recalls Acceleroto's Bryan Duke.

It took updates, good support, and marketing to make it happen. Once *Air Hockey* hit the top 100 games chart, it started marching quickly uphill. I knew then that it had a life of its own. It quickly made it into the top 100 apps.

From there, sales exploded.

The day *Air Hockey* hit the number-one paid game spot, my wife and I were on vacation on Catalina Island off the coast from Los

Angeles. Thanks to the iPhone, we were able to watch the ranking climb. Best vacation *ever*.[35]

This still doesn't reveal anything about the Apple selection process.

It's still a mystery how apps get chosen for the different App Store feature lists. Getting on those lists is the number-one priority of my marketing though [Duke acknowledges]. I once passed an Apple Evangelist on the street in San Francisco and he told me he was just looking at my Web page.

Trust me, you want that to happen.[36]

A Level Playing Field

Existing game developers who had relationships with Apple still need to fight to remain top-of-mind with the company. Even with a head start, everyone needs to prove their worth in this new ecosystem.

Freeverse is a Brooklyn-based Mac game development shop that has recently shifted a lot of its focus to the iPhone platform. When asked how the Apple relationship came to be, Freeverse vice president and cofounder Colin Smith explains:

Fifteen years of making games for the Macintosh! You don't build relationships in a day—they take time. If you build something great, someone at Apple might notice. You'll get a fan, and you'll get a contact. Apple loves design and loves quality, so build with them in-mind and you never know.[37]

Another Mac to iPhone convert, PopCap's John Vechey echoes the sentiment:

Our relationship with Apple started with creating *Bejeweled* and *Zuma* for the scroll-wheel iPods. Both of those were top-selling games on those legacy devices, and so when the iPhone app store rolled out we already had some experience working with them. As far as recommendations on how to become appealing to Apple, my advice would be (1) make products that really sell the coolness of the phone and (2) keep those products exclusive.

Though the iPhone is an open platform, Apple definitely seems to favor companies who focus on their devices.[38]

The most important thing to take into account when trying to establish a relationship with Apple is that you really can't force it, Vechey observes:

> It's tough to explain how we established a relationship with Apple because we didn't do anything to build a relationship with Apple. If they like your app, they will contact you. That's pretty much all there is to it. At least that's how it is for us. We'll just continue to build the best apps we can and hope that Apple will take notice.[39]

That's not to say that you don't have control over what is being presented to Apple. Because, let's face it, even Apple is susceptible to excellent branding. The Iconfactory's Craig Hockenberry got a foot in the door by creating an app so elegant that Apple gave it an award:

> For *Twitterrific,* winning an Apple Design Award was pretty important. With other products, we've done it all in-house. *Ramp Champ* had a great launch because of the buzz we built up before the launch with a teaser promotional site. We have some very talented designers on board, so generating the assets is relatively easy. We've also found that some of the buzz rubs off on Apple—*Ramp Champ* got featured in iTunes both in the "What's Hot" and "New and Noteworthy" sections. Every developer who's been on the front page of iTunes knows how important that spot is![40]

TechCrunch's MG Siegler is among the most prolific bloggers covering the iPhone space in the world. He is arguably the gatekeeper for more app reviews that get picked up by mainstream channels, via syndication through partners such as the *Washington Post,* than anyone else.

"If you're not so lucky to catch Apple's eye, it's always a solid bet simply to create a great app that people not only will want to use, but that the press will find interesting enough to write about," he observes.[41]

How staff picks are selected remains a mystery, but the effect of being chosen is immediately apparent, as *reMovem*'s Matt Martel learned when his app was selected for the honor:

> One of my trivia games, *inFact World,* was featured as a staff pick for three weeks starting February 2, 2008. That turned out to be a huge break, and sales for the game multiplied about twentyfold during that time. It was a real kick to look at the list of top-paid trivia games and see *inFact World* right behind *Deal or No Deal, The Price Is Right, Who Wants to Be a Millionaire,* and ahead of *Smarter Than a Fifth Grader* and *Ben Stein: It's Trivial.* Being listed as a staff pick pushed *inFact World* up among the name brands.
>
> As a side note, I should mention that one of my other games in the *inFact* family—*inFact USA*—rode its coattails to number eighteen of paid trivia games at that time.[42]

Don't Bite the Hand That Feeds You

My best advice to developers looking to get noticed by Apple is to garner media attention but *not* by bashing the company. Developers need to think about the long-term implications of the approach they take with a company that can provide a tremendous platform for their products.

Freeverse vice president and cofounder Colin Smith explains it concisely:

> Apple rewards success. So if you get your app on the charts without them, they might notice. What I would *not* do is start spamming Apple with pleas to feature your app, or whining about the approval process. You want them notice you—but not like that.[43]

Ironically, the developers who rely on the App Store to distribute their wares are the same group who are the first to blame Apple when they are dissatisfied with various aspects related to the iPhone platform. *Wired.com*'s Brian X. Chen has covered most of the high-profile app rejections and tirades against Apple, and he recommends a distinctly positive approach:

> Especially in a tough economy, when [people are] getting laid off left and right, now is a better time than ever to be an independent developer for the iPhone. And a lot of independent developers know that to stand out, they must innovate and write clean code—even better for the iPhone and its users.
>
> A rather interesting circumstance is when a developer stirs controversy related to Apple. For example, his app may have been rejected for a lame reason, giving journalists an opportunity to write critical pieces about Apple. Every company needs a critic. These stories gain a lot more attention than soft gushy articles praising Apple—in the same way that negative articles about death [and] disaster tend to attract more reader attention than positive ones. Kind of shows an ugly side of human nature, but people do enjoy reading about controversy and drama.
>
> I find it fascinating that Apple continues to turn various industries upside down with the iPhone. First the mobile industry, now the mobile software industry; the company already dominates the

digital music space with the iPod. There's plenty Apple has yet to attack with this gadget. Enterprise software is a space Apple is clearly targeting with the new security features introduced in the latest iPhone.

We've reached an era where the importance of software supersedes hardware, and Apple has seen this coming for years. The iPhone . . . keeps getting more powerful with software updates. And by creating a successful business platform for independent developers, Apple has ensured that the capabilities of the iPhone will continue to expand rapidly.[44]

We haven't talked about the iPad much because there simply isn't as much data around the device. However, the iPad provides a tremendous new opportunity to win favor from Apple. The number of apps developed for this device is only a *fraction* of the number available for the iPhone, which means your ability to stand apart is statistically more significant. You have an exponentially greater chance of being selected for one of the App Store's coveted ad spots or App Store promos if you build a really extraordinary iPad application that takes advantage of all the features Apple has provided, and you do so in a memorable way.

Apple is starved for success stories taking place on their new platform, so they can scream it from the rooftops. Be sure you're doing everything you can to increase your visibility.

Insights from a Former iPhone Evangelist

Matt Drance is a very familiar name in the iPhone community. He joined Apple just after the release of Mac OS X and before the introduction of the first iPod. He spent eight years building the Java, Dashboard, and Cocoa developer communities on the Mac, later focusing his energy to help shape the APIs and technologies behind the iPhone SDK. His code is peppered in probably hundreds of third-party products, and his presentations and videos as an Apple evangelist have been viewed by tens of thousands of developers. His work has been demoed in multiple Apple keynote events, and during his time at Apple Matt was a primary coordinator of technical content for the Worldwide Developers Conference.

Matt's excitement about the iPhone OS platform and the opportunity surrounding it led him to leave Apple in 2009 and start his own development business. Bookhouse Software is considered one of the hottest iPhone development shops in the space, and his insights provide a rare glimpse into the thought process behind many of Apple's decisions regarding the App Store.

First he addresses how developers connect with someone at Apple:

In the age of Twitter, Facebook, and rampant blogging, this is easier than it's ever been. Just talk! Promote your stuff *and yourself.* There are plenty of developers who are as well-known for their words as for their products. Never underestimate the power of personal connection. With a blog or a tweet or a YouTube video, you can reach out to Apple employees without even knowing it—until your app is suddenly a staff pick.

You should also go to Apple-hosted events, including WWDC and the iPhone Tech Talks, and introduce yourself to whoever's there.

Finally, if you really believe your product is great, submit it to the Apple Design Awards. ADA submissions are carefully reviewed by a large number of Apple employees, and there are dozens of *great* products every year that don't win. Those products, however, do make an impression on influential people.[45]

How does Apple pick the apps that hold the coveted Apple Staff Picks spots?

Staff Picks are really just that [he says]. Many times it's just the luck of someone in Cupertino thinking your app is great. This underscores the need to keep promoting your app, because you never know who's listening. It never hurts to know people—in this industry as in any—but the app still needs to be cool, thought out, and polished.[46]

So what exactly are the reasons some apps are approved?

Despite the controversial headlines, simple stability remains the number-one reason for rejections [Drance explains]. Test [your app] on every piece of hardware you've marked as supported in iTunes Connect. Don't assume your app works on a first-gen iPod touch because you tested it on a new one, or vice versa. If you don't have access to that hardware, then don't include it in your support matrix. It's neither hard nor expensive to find old hardware these days, so you really have no excuse.

The same goes for software: if you want to expand your audience by supporting earlier OS versions, you had better test those versions before you submit.

Yes, there have been some boneheaded rejections. But they are in the minority, and the policies are rapidly changing. If you're particularly worried about a feature in your app, just make sure you've coded it for easy removal in case there ends up being a problem.[47]

What makes a great app?

I think the best kind of app is one that knows its audience. The developer makes a firm decision on what problem he or she is going to solve and solves that problem well, without flying off in too many directions. Take the time to think about how your users behave, and you make sure your app helps—not hinders—that. As the number of apps continues to skyrocket, truly unique ideas are that much harder to come by. What's left, then, is quality, refinement, and a genuine connection with your user. Only that will protect you from your competition, or, if you're new to the game, empower you to attack it.

The mindless gold rush is over, so if you don't have an exciting idea, keep your day job. However, I absolutely believe there's still room for success—and will be for years to come—if you take the time to really do it right. If you have a truly solid product, then you're bound to have some traction with more than 50 million potential customers and growing out there.

The game can and will change with every new hardware and OS release. There are things Apple can do with the platform tomorrow that would open up an entire new class of applications. And the underlying technology and APIs are so mature and consistent, that when a new developer feature does drop, you learn it in an instant, because it's in the same style and grammar as the stuff you've already learned. The platform is far from exhausted—that's part of what makes this so exciting.[48]

Rankings: The First 48 Hours

As we discussed in the first section, Apple also has been very nebulous around how the App Store rankings work.

It appears, after months of reviewing data and analyzing patterns, that there is a forty-eight-hour window especially critical to the launch of an app. This time period is the perfect storm of building anticipation for launch (which we will discuss later), getting press attention, and, most critical, being featured on the "What's New" list in the App Store.

Most consumers check this list when they first enter the App Store, and sometimes it's a daily activity for iPhone users. That's why this list, which apps are on for a very limited time period, is key to catapulting winning apps to the top of the charts.

People like product launches.

They get excited about being the first in line to try something. If you need proof, stand in front of an Apple store the day a new iPhone is released. Everyone wants to be an early adopter, so don't let that opportunity pass you by. Maximize the viral capacity of your launch and drive the resulting actions to become *conversions*. People share links to the App Store and show off apps to one another. Time your launch so that you have prepared your marketing materials in a way that enables you to capitalize on those first two days.

RunKeeper's Jason Jacobs explains how important the initial launch window is to creating a sustainable buzz around a new app:

> When we first launched, it was August 2008, only a month after the App Store went live. Initial awareness of our app to new users came from press from places like The Unofficial Apple Weblog (TUAW), AppleInsider, TechCrunch, and the *New York Times*. A big breakthrough for us was enabling users to automatically share their activities on Facebook and Twitter just by doing them.
>
> This changed the dynamic for the users in that they were now accountable to their friends and followers and felt more social pressure to run farther and faster. It also changed the dynamic from a marketing standpoint, since tens of thousands of users are now auto-posting every *RunKeeper* activity, which serves as an implicit endorsement of our product and a powerful marketing vehicle to increase viral awareness at no cost to us.[49]

John Vechey of Freeverse believes that in order to launch a successful title, the core group of application pundits must support it:

The launch is the key. Throw everything you've got—ads, interviews, forum posts, email blasts, the kitchen sink—into making sure you get as many downloads as possible in the first few days.[50]

So what does that mean for you? Everyone's capabilities are different, from an entirely "earned media" approach at one end of the spectrum to a primarily advertising-driven launch on the other. My idea of John Vechey's "kitchen sink" is as follows:

- Long-lead press tied up at least three months ahead of the launch
- Highly pertinent but small ad spend (around $5,000–$25,000) in an extremely targeted channel based around your primary audience
- At least one month of prepromotion email and data capture and subsequent email blast one week before the launch
- Forum posts on all pertinent sites, including Apple-centric sites such as MacRumors and AppleInsider
- Interviews with media publications
- Social media presence, primarily on Facebook and Twitter
- Consistent presence on all influencer blogs via comments or contributed articles

Be Patient

The App Store is a brand new ecosystem, and data about consumer purchasing patterns is just beginning to trickle in and take form as "industry best practices." As with any nascent market, the app developers looking to succeed in this space require patience and a willingness to be steadfast in their approach.

A desire for instant gratification has led to a lot of the pricing difficulties we've seen in this community. This is a testament to the fact that we as developers are the only ones who can create an App Store ecosystem of which we are proud to be a part. We're all just learning the best way to create hit applications that garner replicable and predictable success. Remember that even the world's most successful app developers had struggles as they figured out the right mix of messaging, product, and marketing to perform well on the store.

"The first thirty days were really tough," *App Cubby*'s Barnard reveals. "*Trip Cubby* was making just enough to keep the company afloat, but certainly didn't make it clear that *App Cubby* was going to be something worth pouring more time and money into."[51]

Don't rush to build a $20 million company right off the bat. Start slowly, learn quickly, and iterate rapidly.

"Paul and I had day jobs when we started Tapbots," Mark Jardine remembers.

> Since we had steady income outside of the App Store, we felt no pressure to build Tapbots like a traditional company. We made up our own rules, took many risks, and enjoyed every step without the pressures of our little company being the primary source of our income. It allowed us to learn things really quickly. We have yet to hire any outside help and do all the design, development, marketing, and support between the two of us.[52]

Igor Pusenjak of Lima Sky recalls the tumultuous beginnings of his company's wildly successful application, *Doodle Jump:*

> First thirty days post–*Doodle Jump* launch were a roller coaster ride. To our surprise and great disappointment, we sold twenty-one copies the first full day *Doodle Jump* was in the App Store. Second day was no better. We were puzzled because we knew we had a great game. It was clear this one would not sell itself and we needed to do something.
>
> We started emailing every single iPhone game review site, but got almost no response initially. Then suddenly, we saw that Touch Arcade picked up *Doodle Jump* and wrote a positive review. At that

point we were eagerly awaiting the next day to see the sales, only to be disappointed again.

While there certainly was a considerable bump, it was nowhere near what we were hoping for. It was barely enough to keep *Doodle Jump* from falling out of the top 100 in the category "Entertainment" at the time. And then one day, after a lot of emailing, it happened. *Doodle Jump* got featured by Apple in "New and Noteworthy." Except I didn't know about it since I was on vacation at the time in a desert in Morocco!

Talk about timing.

Once I found out, we started a second push of emails. This is when Gizmodo wrote about *Doodle Jump* in its weekly iPhone apps column. The two promotions combined brought *Doodle Jump* to number six "Top Paid Apps" spot on the U.S. App Store in April.

I thought that that was it, and that now that *Doodle Jump* was on top, people would continue to buy it since it was so visible. But, as Apple's promotion ended and Gizmodo's story faded, our sales started to dive.[53]

It was still enough to create a passionate user base of repeat users, though. *Doodle Jump* was rated one of *Wired.com*'s top 20 best iPhone apps of 2009.

Focus on Executing

In a nascent market, the only thing you can control is how hard you're willing to fight to sell your apps. Even without the basics that we take for granted at this stage, in July 2008 developers were pushing forward to create their space in the store.

"For the first several weeks, we had little clue how much our apps were selling, since Apple didn't have daily reporting in place when the App Store first launched," John Casasanta remembers.

We had the *feeling* that we were doing very well since our app, *Where To,* had been ranking very high since the store opened. But we were met with a very pleasant surprise once the numbers finally came in. We sold over 24,000 copies for the first month, netting over $50,000.

But it's amazing to see how the App Store has grown since the early days. While it was possible to break into the top 100 then with maybe 100 sales or so per day, these days, even selling 1,000 per day won't keep you in the top 100. It's kind of crazy to think about when you consider that a developer of a Mac app is very fortunate to see double-digit sales numbers for their apps on a typical day.[54]

Don't let a lack of resources be your scapegoat for not putting out the best app possible with the best marketing you can manage.

App Cubby has never had any employees. I contract out the coding, design, tech support, and pretty much everything else I can. That makes it sound like I don't do anything, but it's actually one of the keys to *App Cubby*'s success. Hiring talented professionals [on a free-lance basis] to do things outside my core competencies allowed me to focus on the thing I'm best at—app producer—and gave me time to learn more about marketing and other aspects of running a business.[55]

Tweetie: A Marketing Case Study

With more than 300,000 apps available in the App Store, it's exceedingly difficult to stand out. But there are some rare cases when the stars align, and, more important, when a developer is prepared with all the pieces necessary to create a runaway success and win market share overnight.

Tweetie is an app that, whether the developer was aware of it or not, took in all the concepts presented in this book and executed flawlessly. In a world inundated with Twitter apps, Loren Brichter, founder of AteBits, was able to break through the noise and claim a position in the marketplace. *Tweetie* continues to be one of the most talked about, written about, and downloaded apps in the App Store's history. Brichter's app has been acquired by Twitter and is now the official Twitter for iPhone application:

> I may be an outlier, but I didn't do any typical "business stuff" before launching anything. One day I was playing with my iPhone, and asking myself why every Twitter client I tried was so sluggish. I figured I could write my own, so I did. Two weeks later, I gave it to a few friends, spent a week fixing some bugs, and submitted it to the App Store. Two weeks after that Apple approved it.
>
> I made almost $1,000 the day it launched. Then sales dropped to nothing, but I didn't care because I wasn't making any money at the time anyway and $1,000 was a lot of money and definitely covered the two weeks of effort that went into it.[56]

Brichter is humble, but he did jump on the media and marketing opportunities presented to him and as a result stayed top-of-mind to the media, the iPhone development community, and consumers:

> *Tweetie* was just a side project—a way to get my feet wet with iPhone app development. I wrote it for me, and it was fun. So I released a few updates, and sales slowly crept up a bit. And I got lucky with some well-timed press, a high-profile rejection story, and of course, PEE [Brichter's parody product for achieving a high ranking in the App Store]. And sales jumped a bit more.
>
> I did get lucky breaks with press a few times. The "censorship" rejection fiasco boosted sales, as did the introduction of PEE. Once the app was already popular, it sort of drove its own growth . . . I guess once you hit some "critical mass" you'll get featured by Apple,

which in turn will make it more popular, which in turn will get you featured elsewhere, etc.

I don't remember when it happened, one day I realized I was making a living selling *Tweetie*. I never expected it to happen, but figured I'd ride the wave as long as it lasted. So I put my head down and got to work, releasing a slew of updates, revamping some internal stuff, launching *Tweetie* for Mac, and most recently, *Tweetie 2* for iPhone. *Tweetie 1* had a spike at the beginning, then fell off to nothing. The *Tweetie 2* graph actually looks very similar, if you scale it vertically a bit and rather than fall off to nothing, it falls off to a nice living.

Writing a Twitter client is cheating a bit though—if the app is any good, it'll market itself. Those little links on Twitter.com under tweets (e.g., five minutes ago from *Tweetie*) account for close to 50 percent of referrals to atebits.com.

I guess my strategy would boil down to:

1. Write a good app.
2. Charge for it.

If you do that and aren't doing well, I'd go back and make sure you really nailed step 1 and [that] the market you're targeting actually exists.

Having a popular app certainly gets Apple's attention, they'll probably reach out to you eventually. I'm not sure if there's any magic to it, but it's always helpful to remember that you're dealing with really caring, dedicated people over there who are still working out the kinks in this crazy amazing new system. It's too easy to get frustrated, but if you're writing an iPhone app you've probably already come to the conclusion that this is the best game in town— by a long shot, in my humble opinion—and it's only getting better. I'm not 100 percent sure how to keep my brand out front. I just keep writing the best software I can. I can't say my approach has been the most profitable because I have no way to compare it, but my goal has never been to grow a strong brand or gobble up market share, it's been focused almost exclusively on improving the product itself. I think that's what it's all about.

I'm sure others can do a much better job than me accelerating adoption and growing brands, and improving market share and all that stuff, but at some point, it's about the product.[57]

Marketing Workout

For this chapter's workout, let's focus on flexing your brand awareness of companies you admire. What about these companies and products resonates with you? What can you take away from your responses and apply to your product's marketing program?

Dig deep; your answers to these questions will help define and shape your brand identity.

Name five companies with whose philosophies you agree:

_____

_____

_____

_____

_____

_____

_____

_____

How do they communicate their philosophies?

_____

_____

_____

_____
_____
_____
_____
_____
_____

Name five companies with whose philosophies you *disagree:*

_____
_____
_____
_____
_____
_____
_____
_____

How do they communicate their philosophies?

_____
_____
_____
_____
_____
_____
_____
_____

What does your company stand for?

_____
_____
_____

_____
_____
_____
_____
_____
_____

How can you express your company's philosophy to someone who doesn't know you?

_____
_____
_____
_____
_____
_____
_____
_____
_____

What aspect of your company does your app represent?

_____
_____
_____
_____
_____
_____
_____
_____

How can you put that into words?

_____
_____

_____
_____
_____
_____
_____
_____
_____

What is the most exciting part of developing your app?

_____
_____
_____
_____
_____
_____
_____
_____

How can you put that into words?

_____
_____
_____
_____
_____
_____
_____
_____

List some examples of apps that depend on the time of the year for success.

_____
_____

_____

_____

_____

_____

_____

_____

_____

Does your app fall into this category? If so, when would it seem best to release your app?

_____

_____

_____

_____

_____

_____

_____

_____

What are the prices of apps similar to yours?

_____

_____

_____

_____

_____

_____

_____

Which of those apps do you consider to be of quality?

_____

_____

_____

_____

_____

_____

_____

_____

_____

_____

Which of those apps enjoy the image you would want for your app?

_____

_____

_____

_____

_____

_____

_____

_____

_____

Have you ever bought an app as a result of advertising?
☐ Yes　☐ No

Where do you learn about the apps you purchase?

_____

_____

_____

_____

_____

_____

_____

_____

_____

Would you prefer to promote your app by:

☐ Dressing as a giant iPhone and running in a marathon?

☐ Dressing in a bunny suit and hopping through Times Square?

☐ Becoming the world's first iPad DJ?

☐ Jumping naked out of an airplane?

What was the most entertaining promotion you've seen for an app?

_____

_____

_____

_____

_____

_____

_____

_____

Did you buy the app?

☐ Yes ☐ No

What social networking sites do you use?

_____

_____

_____

_____

_____

_____

What social networking sites do you use for discussing the iPhone, iPad, and their apps?

_____

_____

_____

_____

_____

_____

_____

_____

_____

How does your app make the iPhone or iPad look good?

_____

_____

_____

_____

_____

_____

_____

_____

What traits have caused apps to be selected for the spotlight in the App Store, or given awards?

_____

_____

_____

_____

_____

_____

_____

_____

_____

What is it about your app that will cause it to receive that sort of attention?

_____

_____

_____

_____

_____

_____

_____

_____

_____

Great job! Now you're halfway through the book. Not so bad, right?

This stuff isn't scary when you break it down into bite-sized pieces. Now that you know how to position and how to bring your product to market, let's talk about execution and reaching out to your customers and to the media.

Let's go!

4

Outreach

Long before there were public relations firms and branding consultants and social media outreach teams, there were people who were trying to be noticed by their peers. Today the mobile era makes it possible for those people to produce and sell killer apps, and *really* grab attention.

But it takes legwork.

First-time publicists shouldn't be intimidated by the idea of doing public relations, though. Just think about it from a practical perspective.

PR Doesn't Have to Be Scary

In the public relations world, there are certain benchmarks by which success is typically measured. In a market as new as the iPhone app space, these benchmarks haven't yet been identified and secured, so innovation is still possible.

Although it's typically considered the holy grail of press attention, coverage on a national TV show may not move the needle on app sales. Todd Moore, developer of the wildly popular app *White Noise*, told the story of how a minute-long segment on *Late Night with Jimmy Fallon,* mocking his app, had virtually no effect on his sales!

That's hard to believe, but he has the data to support it. And while it's possible that these brand impressions may have translated to sales at some point farther down the road, the reality is that a high-profile media hit didn't immediately influence his sales figures.

On the other hand, a brief notice on an app review site may send sales skyrocketing. So if the traditional rules don't necessarily apply, you have the opportunity—even the incentive—to be *non*traditional when doing your own PR.

You Don't Need a Fancy PR Firm

Interestingly, most of the independent developers I've interviewed tell similar stories concerning their media outreach initiatives. Indies are typically having a great deal of success in playing publicist to their own products. This is a great sign, because it shows that those in the media are willing to take calls and interview one-man development shops, weighing their opinions much the same as those of the huge developers with millions of dollars in venture capital.

Thinking of it with this perspective makes it much less intimidating to small developers who may find themselves engaging the media.

Everyone out there craves information about the App Store and wants to know what the developers experience while building atop the platform. If you have a unique story or perspective on current events, the media wants to talk to you!

Public relations for your app is simpler than you think.

In fact, simple is *better*—you can become paralyzed by making your PR plan too complex. And don't let it be an excuse for inaction, either. Many first-time marketers seem to "not bother" because they believe they won't be able to execute the perfect PR plan, or because they don't have a reputable publicist helping them.

"Marketing is extremely important to ensure the success of an app," *Wired.com*'s Brian X. Chen says. "But not in the traditional sense. Some independent coders have become successful by simply blogging about their app, or pitching it to journalists. There are plenty of different ladders developers can climb for doing their own marketing."[1]

Jason Jacobs of *RunKeeper* echoes the sentiment:

I've done most of it myself up to this point. We do plan to eventually get additional in-house help in this area as we grow, but it is critical that when we do, the user communications maintain the same style, responsiveness, and feel that have gotten us to where we are now.

Like many small developers, everything I've done for marketing strategy was in-house and done as a side-job to development and other business functions. Using a firm that is 100 percent marketing would be wonderful, but it's out of reach for many developers.

Still, think big. Just do it smartly and within your means.[2]

Sometimes hiring a public relations firm won't give you the results you're looking for. "We hired a PR firm last year for MacHeist and the results were beyond dismal," tap tap tap's John Casasanta recounts.

We've been able to secure much better media placement on our own over the years. Save your money.

Lately, we don't even bother sending out press releases for anything. The media coverage that it nets simply can't compare to what we're able to do on our own through the combination of jointly promoting via tap tap tap and MacHeist.[3]

But before you abandon the idea of PR altogether, remember that not every situation is identical. "We're in a bit of an atypical situation compared to most other developers," Casasanta admits, "so take this with a grain of salt."[4]

Identify Relevant Audiences and Where They Live

Location, location, *location.*

This doesn't just apply to real estate. Before you can identify the media you're going to approach, there are even *more* basic things you need to determine.

Where is your audience found: the people who *read* the articles and reviews and will buy your app?

And how can you reach them? A significant portion of the questionnaire you filled out in Chapter 2 was built around the profiles and behaviors of those who might be your potential customers. Understanding who your audience is gives you insights into the tools you need in order to reach them most effectively.

Are the people who will buy your app women aged twenty-four to thirty-five? Do they read fashion publications? If that's the case, then you can find out which publications you need to engage in order to reach that audience segment.

The media pays attention to buzz. If you're not sure of where to start, think about the feedback you would get if you were to survey your users. Who loves you the most?

Start there.

Knowing your audience is especially important because, in a major shift since the beginnings of the App Store, your application now has a lifespan beyond the initial purchase point. It used to be that if you sold an app, that was it—the revenue stream died there. Now there are subscriptions and in-app purchases, so gaining a user may mean recruiting a lifetime fan and consumer. These are relationships that will continue long after the user has downloaded your app.

In fact, in the greatest app success stories consumers have felt rewarded over the lifetime of use, and built up word-of-mouth marketing. A lot has been said about success through evangelism, but before you can build a fan base, you need to know where your potential fans prefer to learn about new products.

The media will follow the buzz.

Understanding where your audience gets its news and information lets you track where the conversions to app downloads are happening. Are they coming from links?

From the Web to the app?
On specific devices?
On iTunes?

Knowing this can help you home in on the publications, blogs, websites, and other media most critical for you to reach.

Reach Out to the Reporters

The key is to give the media what it's looking for. No one wants to cover the same story over and over, and writers are always looking for something fresh and interesting.

"Don't reinvent the wheel," *Wired.com*'s Chen says.

Use your imaginations and blow us away with something fresh and cool. This new iPhone should spawn some multimedia-savvy apps. Video and multimedia messaging is mostly popular among smartphone users in Japan; the iPhone is going to make the entire world multimedia-savvy.

Think along those lines to create something exciting.[5]

Don't be shy! No one can write about your incredibly cool app if they don't know it exists. Igor Pusenjak of Lima Sky realized the importance of proactive outreach, and was able to secure some impressive coverage as a result:

We had been emailing every site that writes about iPhone games. We believed we had a great game on our hands and did our best to relay that in the emails. As *Doodle Jump* became more popular, more of the media started to take notice. *Doodle Jump* got mentioned on CBS's *The Big Bang Theory,* played on air on a popular UK radio station, and was proclaimed their obsession and favorite game by the Jonas Brothers.[6]

But sending press materials to every media outlet is going to take forever, and your return will never live up to the blood, sweat, and tears you put into it. *Target* your efforts to the outlets that are most likely to yield results, then stretch a little further. It doesn't hurt to take a few chances—getting Al Roker to gush about your app is a long shot, but worth the effort.

Of course, there are some media outlets every developer needs to address; they form the core of app journalism. This is where I would begin if I were beginning my outreach today.

Blogs like Pocket Gamer, Macrumors, 148apps, AppleInsider, TUAW, and App Craver focus much of their content around app reviews, and lots of users check these sites regularly to learn about the newest and best apps. Because of the niche nature of these publications, they are often very open to unsolicited pitches, and most post an email address for press releases on their sites.

Make sure you include these folks in every mailing.

Short and Sweet

For the same reasons reporters don't want you to waste their time with meaningless chatter, they also want your press releases to be short and to the point.

"By short, I mean less than two paragraphs total," Wilson Tang of CNET explains.

> I want to know almost immediately what your app does and a little about yourself or your company. Again, keep it short! I cannot stress that enough. If you cannot pitch me your app in three sentences or less, then something is wrong with your pitch—and likely your app.[7]

Most important, be prepared with the necessary materials when you're reaching out.

> I'm not going to pay for your app just to try it out [Tang continues]. Give us a promo code and a link to the app in the iTunes store.
>
> Please have a press kit ready for your app. In pragmatic terms, that means *don't* send a giant un-editable, uncopyable PDF file. Reporters and journalists want to craft their own story. The best thing you can do for them is make your photos, videos, descriptions, and biographies easily accessible to them to post to a blog or encode in a video.[8]

Be real.

> By far the most irritating thing PR people do is smile through their teeth and overlook every single defect or shortcoming of their product [Tang explains]. Being honest about everything gets you a lot of credibility with a journalist. Just because your app doesn't have feature "B" and "C" doesn't mean that it doesn't do feature "A" exceptionally well, and that might actually be the story that a reporter wants to tell.[9]

The most common question I'm asked about PR is how to format a press release. Here is how I go about writing a release:

Subject: **Announcing iMockups, a gorgeous, rapid wireframing and layout app designed exclusively for the iPad.**

Hi,

We know you folks are super busy so we'll keep this app description short and sweet.

Endloop is proud to announce iMockups, a gorgeous, rapid wireframing and layout app designed exclusively for the iPad.

- Designed for rapid creation of mock-ups, layouts and wireframes for your web, iPhone and iPad projects.
- Low fidelity mockups help you, your team and your clients focus on functionality and flow.
- Get creative with our ever expanding variety of smart customizable UI controls like navbars, tab panels, and our favorite, an autofilling Lorem Ipsum block.
- The gorgeous interface not only makes it a joy to look and touch, it's designed to let you work the way you want. Panels easily slide out of the way when you don't need them.
- Collaborate and discuss your designs quickly and easily with full-screen Presentation mode.
- Supports multiple projects and multiple pages per project keep your projects organized
- Expect fast and furious updates that include new controls and features.

YouTube video link (35 seconds only, best viewed at 480p): http://www.youtube.com/watch?v=LOyIVqJcGfc

Attached are 2 screenshots of iMockup. You can also access all 5 screenshots here: http://www.endloop.ca/press

iMockups is currently "In Review" and was submitted in time for the iPad App Store grand opening event.

Thanks for your consideration and time.

For your reference:
Endloop's website: http://www.endloop.ca
Our Blog: http://blog.endloop.ca

Regards,

_____

Garry Seto
Co-Founder, Endloop Studios

_____

Keep it short and sweet. Reporters don't like long press releases and they really don't like exaggeration. Don't inflate your news. If you write a press release and by the time you're done you realize it isn't newsworthy, then *don't put it out.* If you bombard the media with trivial news stories and small incremental changes in your company or product, they may ignore you when something *really* important comes along.

Save your press release for compelling news and customer wins that genuinely mark significant growth and progress for your business.

Determine Angles

There's another very important thing to understand before we dive into creating an angle for your app.

Most writers aren't iPhone developers. In fact, most have never written code.

Writers are communicators and, in a sense, storytellers. In order to convince them that you have a tale to tell, you *must* be able to create a unique and engaging story around your app. This is what I mean by identifying an angle.

It's an extension of the positioning statement you created earlier. For example, if you built an app called *Closest Cup* that locates nearby coffee shops, your angle could be that it is "the only app on the market that tracks coffee shops in cities and gives you turn-by-turn directions showing how to get there." In theory, this is something unique, compelling, and interesting that may pique a writer's interest in covering your app.

(Especially if he's a coffee junkie.)

One of the best representations of having a solid angle in the App Store belongs to the application *Bump*. The idea is that *Bump* lets you connect two mobile phones by just "bumping" them together.

"The idea for *Bump* came out of personal frustration at having to manually type contact information into my phone," David Lieb, CEO of Bump Technologies recalls.

> The idea came on day one, and we started building the product on day two. Today, the *Bump* app lets you exchange contact information, share photos, and compare friends on iPhone and Android devices.[10]

With a compelling angle built into the functionality of the app, Lieb and his team were able to drum up media interest despite the fact that they had no experience in doing PR:

> The day the app launched, one of my cofounders and I just emailed every person we know, and reached out to a few bloggers we'd met. Fortunately, *Bump* is a pretty novel and tangible technology that people seem to like to talk about.
>
> One thing led to another, and our download numbers grew. We got a couple of TV segments, which helped the buzz further snow-

ball. In April, we happened to become the billionth app downloaded on the iTunes App Store, and in August, Apple featured us in an iPhone TV commercial.[11]

In truth, *Bump*'s media pickup exceeded any anticipation the team might have had.

> The first month was wild [Lieb recalls]. We had no idea anyone would go for this new form of interaction. We thought it had a chance to catch on, but we really had low expectations. Seeing people start to use *Bump,* and tell their friends about it, was really exciting.
>
> We've never really focused on generating media attention. We'd prefer to spend that time making a cool product, and letting our users get the attention of the media. Besides, the whole purpose of media attention is to spread the word to users, right? Sometime during the first month, we re-ran all our analytics. One of the really interesting stats was the degree to which people were encouraging their friends to download the app and use it right there on the spot. Seeing how high that number was gave us good confidence that *Bump* had a chance to spread virally.[12]

And once again, success boiled down to the quality of the core product.

> *Bump* is unique in the sense that it takes two people to use [Lieb adds]. When someone new gets the app and tries it, they are then compelled to tell their friends about it, if for no other reason than to make the app more useful for themselves. This—combined with the fact that *Bump* is simple, somewhat magical, and fun—helps to keep the word about *Bump* spreading.[13]

TechCrunch's MG Siegler, who covers a lot of the top-performing apps in the App Store, is also known for breaking stories about apps.

His coverage can make or break an app's reputation, and he receives hundreds of PR requests from developers each day.

> I like to receive information about new apps mainly by word-of-mouth [Siegler reveals]. That always seem to be the best indicator if an app is actually going to be good or not. Apple's own picks are usually pretty solid, [and] being the first to know about an app helps, as well. Be brief and explain clearly what the app does. Videos and pictures always help, as apps are very visual things.[14]

In addition to word-of-mouth recommendations, Siegler does pay attention to notices he receives from more conventional sources:

> It seems like some PR companies are more comfortable taking on more "extreme" apps and noting how controversial they are in an attempt to get writers to cover them. I'm also noticing PR companies latching on in a big way to certain trends—location, right now, for example—and bombarding my inbox with apps related to that. Both of those seem to be working, to some extent.[15]

His primary advice to developers looking for coverage? Not surprisingly, it's a recurring theme in this book:

> As always, the most important thing is to build a killer app. If you do that, more likely than not, the attention, both from the press and the public, will follow. A lot of the other stuff is random, but you can't go wrong with a great app.[16]

Execution Is Key

Mark Jardine of Tapbots developed a system for launching apps that has worked well for his company:

Our marketing process is fairly simple. Our goal is to come out of the gates running. [Until then] we are very quiet about what our next app will be. We want the news of our new app to be spread on release day. That means being on all the big blogs and websites and people spreading the word on Twitter.

So how do we accomplish this? Well, one way is to get key people ad hoc versions of our app before it's available on the store. This is much harder to do if your company is new or just unknown. It wasn't until our second and third apps that this was an option for us. Alongside regular beta testers, we ask key bloggers and people with Twitter influence if they want to check out an upcoming app.

So far we've been lucky and most—if not all—the people we contact are interested. If someone has no interest in the app, there's no loss. However those who *are* interested can't wait to talk about the app and usually have a blog post/review ready when we launch. If you have a great app, people will spread the word. Our customer's voice is our marketing strategy. The key is to get those with the biggest influence to help spread the word.[17]

But there's more to it than just getting the word out:

We don't want to trick people into buying our app. We want our customers to love what we are building. They are the ones who will help us make our products even better because they really care. And they are the ones who will gladly tell their friends to buy our app.[18]

For Jardine, light advertising also works to augment his PR process:

We also experiment with ad placement, but we don't spend a lot of money on advertising. We place ads on the Fusion Ads network because they are fairly affordable, their audience fits our target market well, and we like their ad philosophy. We've also started experimenting with Facebook Ads.

A nice promotional screenshot and video can go a long way to get attention. We reach out to every media outlet we can think of. We usually send them an email with a screenshot, a one- to two-sentence description of the app, a URL for more info, a promo code, and a link to the video. These guys don't have any time for BS. You have about three seconds to interest them before they hit the "delete" key. A nice screenshot is our hook with more info easily accessible for them.

It's hit and miss, but has been fairly successful for us overall.

Finally, I should mention that *localization* is extremely important to the success of our apps. The U.S. store is a very competitive market. We've done fairly well there, but not as well as we have in the other countries. Our first two apps have hit number-one top paid status multiple times in the other big markets. We always launch with support for at least three to four languages. Not every country will have lighter apps and friends hogging up the top 100.

The U.S. is the biggest market, but it isn't the only market.[19]

While you need to make sure all the essentials are in place, be sure to get creative with your outreach. There are many apps vying for a limited number of stories the media will carry, and being targeted will help your chances in obtaining media coverage. David Barnard of App Cubby looks for as many clever and relevant opportunities as possible to get in front of the press:

The press is completely inundated by promo codes, review requests, and full-on PR spam. That being the case, I've done my best to send very short, relevant messages . . . For example, I saw on Twitter that a particular writer had just purchased a new car. I sent an email saying something like: "Hey, I just saw your tweet about buying a car. I'm the developer of *Gas Cubby*, an iPhone app designed to track and optimize your fuel economy and remind you about maintenance. Here's a promo code, let me know what you think."

If that writer didn't care about fuel economy or maintenance, I didn't waste his time or mine in writing a novel about how great my app is. And if he did care, he probably appreciated that I didn't waste his time, and [might] quickly move on to actually installing *Gas Cubby.*

In all my marketing efforts I do my best to keep communication—via email, phone, in-person, Twitter, Facebook, ads, etc.—meaningful. You'll burn more bridges than you cross by incessantly pitching yourself and/or your product without offering something of meaning.[20]

Be careful when implementing your plans!

Lots of mistakes can be made while executing PR, so everything you do will carry risks. But you will only become comfortable with doing PR by, well, doing PR. *Not* doing so will be far worse.

Some of the mistakes I'll warn you about seem so silly—but trust me—these mistakes are *so common* that they've become red flags for sloppy companies. When you reach out to the media:

1. Spell the reporter's name right. *Ugh.*
2. When preparing a draft, don't leave items blank and think you'll remember to fill them in before you send out the release. At some point you *won't* remember, and you *will* regret it.
3. Don't send an email blast and cc everyone. *Double ugh.* Big no-no. Each release needs to be individually targeted.
4. Don't copy and paste an email with a blank for the reporter's name. The reporter will be very, very upset. Pay close individual attention to each communication.

The lesson here is that you are cultivating an important relationship with those who are writing about your app and your company. Take the time to personalize the outreach you do. Don't rush it. This is your first impression. Make it the right one.

Let Your Fans Be Your Fans and the Media Will Notice

Apps like *RunKeeper*, which have taken the social component into account from the beginning of the development process, are able to build passionate fan bases that can be leveraged into garnering outside media attention.

"For us, the app has always been one input into a larger *RunKeeper* system that we're building," Jason Jacobs explains.

> And while it has come a long way, it is still only the beginning and we have a whole lot left to do and prove. But there have been some moments along the way that have made us realize that we may have something special here.
>
> Most of these moments all come back to the strength and passion of the user community. A few examples of this include when the users nominated us to be finalists in the Mashable OpenWebAwards for "Best Location-Based Mobile App." And then, with a month of voting, several hundred of them volunteered to be notified to go back and vote for us every signal day, and the result was that we won, beating out *foursquare*, Google Maps, and *Gowalla* in the process.
>
> Our user forum is an incredibly vibrant place, where users give us tons of feedback, feature requests, support issues, and many of them help maintain the forum and answer questions for others. They don't just give us a feature here or there, but write many paragraphs about what they want to see, since they care and they are invested in helping *RunKeeper* to become everything that they—and we—want it to be.
>
> Another big break was when we partnered with a group of college students at Emerson College to run a social media campaign around the Boston Marathon involving me running the marathon dressed

as a giant iPhone with *RunKeeper* on the screen. We launched a series of viral videos leading up to the event, and by the time the race was over, it was a global sensation on Twitter, and was covered by dozens of major media outlets including the *New York Times, AdWeek, PRWeek,* Mashable, and many others.

Users who see their friends post about using competitive products on places like Twitter and Facebook jump all over their friends about switching to *RunKeeper.* It is a die-hard and loyal user base, which in itself won't get us to scale, but is a powerful springboard to help get us over the initial hump and buy us time to make the product everything that it can be.[21]

Social Media Is Your Friend

"In the early days of the App Store, it was possible to get by without spending any money on marketing since the number of apps was low, and the interest for them was high," Igor Pusenjak of Lima Sky recalls.

At that time, you could put anything out and it would sell. However, as the App Store became more crowded, it was becoming obvious that in order to succeed one would need to focus more on traditional methods of marketing.

We looked—and to this day are continuing to look for ad buys that would generate an acceptable level of return, and have so far found [almost] none.

So we had to consider other options that would give our products exposure without costing a lot of—or any—money. This is where Facebook and Twitter came in really handy.[22]

Mark Jardine of Tapbots echoes the sentiment:

Twitter is an amazing thing. With every launch we use http://search. twitter.com with the correct search terms in place, sit back and watch the world interact with our new app. We get a good sense how we are doing based on the real-time results. It's very exciting. With Twitter, we know if we have a hit or a flop within hours. Luckily, we've had positive results with all three apps. I should mention that the results have grown exponentially with each release.

Twitter is vital to our marketing strategy.[23]

Try searching for your app name on Twitter. See what comes up. You may be surprised by the robust conversation you find taking place around your app.

Create a Twitter account for your app and engage in conversations with your fans. If someone encounters a bug or has a problem, address it in public for everyone to see. Let your fans see that you're paying attention and you want to create the best experience possible for them.

Don't underestimate the power of customer service carried out using social media.

Naveen Selvadurai of *foursquare* attributes much of his app's success in the App Store to his company's social media savvy. The function of *foursquare* allowed social networking to be built in, so the very *use* of the app offered marketing benefits:

To build up our friend networks initially—which is very important in an app like ours—we built Twitter/Facebook/Gmail hooks early on. We wanted to make it as easy as possible to import our social connections from existing sites. We also made it very easy [for you] to add a friend when you're out and about: when you meet someone at a bar or a conference or something, it's super easy to just drop their phone into our app to immediately connect with them.[24]

Due to the location-based and social media elements, many people use *foursquare* as a replacement for exchanging business cards, and this has fueled a lot of the app's early growth.

"Twitter was great for getting the word out about everything we were working on," Selvadurai recounts.

It was also great to use that as a way to push out content about what our users were doing. We built different messages:

- Ones that got sent to Twitter and Facebook every time you checked in
- Ones that got sent every time you took over mayorship or earned a badge, etc.

We also built in another clever hook. We realized that often times when people tweet, they'll say something like "having a coffee at Think Coffee w/ @soandso" so we decided to let the app automatically populate tweets with the "w/ @soandso."

The more of these users started sending out, the more their friends noticed and—in the same way friends saw mentions of check-ins and mayorships—venues and brands also started noticing all this great conversation on Twitter. Venue owners started seeing that their best customers were using this thing called *foursquare* to talk about their place on Twitter. They started to pay even more attention and began doing things with us.[25]

"Word-of-mouth—or 'word-of-Twitter'—is a huge driver," *Los Angeles Times* writer Mark Milian says. "In order to make something that spreads, it needs to be great or gimmicky enough that people want to talk about it at bars or in cyberspace.[26]

Position *Yourself* as a Product, Too

Another way to get noticed by the media is to become an expert—or at least be seen as one. The media *loves* experts and gurus. But you need to deliver *consistently,* or they'll find another celebrity.

Identify the things you're best able to discuss. For example, if you're good at assessing and discussing sales rankings and pricing strategy, let it be known. Address these topics in all your press releases, blog posts—everything you send out, relating them to the context of the discussion. Thus, when bloggers and writers are looking for this type of information, you become a convenient and reliable resource upon which they can call.

The more you become identified with a specific topic, the more reporters will bookmark your blog, calling upon you on slow news days or when a related topic becomes news.

Make it easy for them to find you, and try to help reporters do their job better by providing commentary, data, and good information.

CNET's Wilson Tang provides sage advice from the perspective of someone who is constantly pitched story ideas by app developers:

> The best approach . . . is to cultivate a good relationship with the media. Reach out to them. Be open with them. Go to mixers. Go to events and conferences. Buy them a drink. Give them a scoop about your buddy's secret Facebook-killer. And they will reward you with ink.[27]

Since most of the industry media are located in New York or San Francisco, it will be best for you to be based in one of those two cities, as well. But if that's not possible, you can reach out to them at trade shows and conferences, and you can make certain your point of view is well represented on your blog, in your press releases, and in all communications with the media.

The best way to engage reporters is word of mouth or email [Tang advises]. First, Twitter the Hell out of your app. If you're going to contact the media, please do not call them. Unless, that is, you know them personally, of course. The industry is stressful enough that getting accosted every few minutes over the phone is *incredibly* annoying, and bad for your reputation. Word spreads quickly that someone is annoyingly hawking their product. Instead, send a short email.[28]

Wearing Two Hats: Developer and Reporter

Henry Balanon is respected in the developer community because he can write about iPhone development from the perspective of an actual developer. He and his partner, John Ellenich, develop apps under the moniker Bickbot. Balanon writes for the GigaOM network blog The Apple Blog and often speaks at conferences regarding public relations for iPhone apps. I wanted to dig into best practices and unearth tips for first-time app publicists.

Search Google or Twitter to figure out who's talking about similar competing apps [Balanon says]. You can identify the personas of your potential audience once you know who's blogging or talking about competing apps.[29]

But don't stop with identifying your primary audience.

You can have multiple secondary audiences, as well [Balanon advises]. You don't have to target just one. Take a look at the *Outside* app for weather. You might think that your audience is just "people who want to know the weather forecast." But it could also be "graphic designers who are obsessed with beautiful interfaces."[30]

This next piece of advice is the most important in identifying your target audience.

"'Everyone' is not a relevant audience," he explains, warning developers not to cast too wide a net.

If you market to everybody, then you sell to nobody.

Think of your stories first. There's a difference between a fitness app and a fitness app that helped Jared lose 500 pounds: One won't get ink and one will. And don't always target the first-tier sites. Sure you might get lucky sometimes, but the *New York Times* or TechCrunch won't care about your app unless it's extraordinary— saves lives, first of its kind, flies planes—or [is] backed by a name they know—EA, ngmoco, Google.

A better way to climb the ranks is to target a second or third tier blog like *Touch Arcade* or *TUAW.* These are the blogs that the big boys read and it's easier to get coverage—assuming your story is solid. Also, go to conferences like WWDC and have beers with the media. Build a relationship with them. It won't guarantee coverage, but at least you'll be able to get on their radar when the time comes.

Your main goal is to catch Apple's attention, so if your app and the story fits, try to target sites that a techie would read. More specifically, what an *Apple* techie would read. The iPhone is unique in that the people who make the product are also fans of the product. Try to target what they might read and maybe one day you'll see yourself on the featured page.

Some of the sites you likely will want to target are:

- Wired.com
- Daring Fireball
- Macworld
- Ars Technica

- Engadget
- Gizmodo

When you do, the important thing to remember is that, while you have information you need to deliver, they need to run stories that will be compelling to their audience.

> First think about the story on why you made the app in the first place [Balanon advises]. What were your frustrations? What problem did you solve? Talk to your beta testers [or current users] and get specific examples on how they use [your app]. Your story gets ink if one of your users saves lives because of your app, or you raised $100K for charity because of your app. What are the "wow" factors about your app that no one else has? Include those in your angle as well. Why does your app blow everything else out of the water? Questions like this need to be answered to craft a good angle.
>
> Launch is key. Keep the buzz light a month before. Start making contact two weeks before approval to get on media radars and give them early access. Send reminders a week before, and another [round] when the app hits the store.[31]

Attend Conferences

Nothing can top face-to-face interaction with reporters. A writer can sense enthusiasm and belief in the product that's being pitched, which can open up and lead to opportunities that would be lost by email exchanges.

Bryan Duke, developer of *Air Hockey*, champions this sentiment:

> All of my media attention so far has been handled in-house. It's been a tough road though. I'm not a born and bred marketing wiz,

so I've had to do a lot of learning as I went. Probably the most important things I've done that helped get my app noticed were shake lots of hands—in person if at all possible—and help others. There's a huge tendency among game developers to be extremely secretive. When it comes to marketing, spending time outside of the office has paid off hugely.

Take WWDC, for example. At the last WWDC, I spent a ton of time meeting people at parties and events after the normal work day. Building real relationships with people around the industry has become the cornerstone of making my marketing happen. Meet everyone you can, not just those who you think can help you directly. People know if you're just hype generating. Find something other than writing code to talk about. Make friends.[32]

But don't attend the events unprepared. Target those in the media you'd like to talk to before you get there. When choosing an event to attend, read the biographies of the panelists and determine if anyone from your target media list will be moderating or speaking on a panel. This will help you shape the angle you'll need when you do speak with that particular writer. Each publication is looking for different things, and being prepared can make or break your pitch.

Come prepared with all the materials you need in order to demo and talk about your app.

Don't get caught off guard, because you never know when the opportunity will arise to talk to a reporter.

"I have handled all of the media relations myself thus far," *RunKeeper*'s Jason Jacobs explains.

One big break was when I was attending the TechCrunch50 Conference in September 2008, one month after we launched. I had arranged before I got there to give one of the TechCrunch writers a demo, and once I did, a few days later we were covered in both

TechCrunch and the *New York Times,* since he was also a writer there.[33]

John Wilker of 360iDev hosts one of the industry's best iPhone developer conferences, working with his partner Tom Ortega. An annual event, 360iDev is considered the indie version of WWDC. Many of the top developers and reporters covering the space attend 360iDev for a glimpse into the next generation of apps slated to be built for iPhone. "I think standing-out in the App Store starts long before your app in submitted to Apple," Wilker explains.

> Events like 360iDev and WWDC, where hundreds and thousands of developers come together to geek out, are where it starts. Once you're in the App Store the connections you made at events and in the community come into play. Getting other developers, press, reviewers, and even event organizers to help make noise and link to your app is crucial.
>
> The old saying makes sense here: if a tree falls in the forest and no one is around to hear it, does it make noise? It's your job to make sure there's someone—lots of someone's if you can manage it—there to hear it.
>
> The App Store is decidedly crowded, but it's not impossible to shine and be seen. Look at *Geo Defense Swarm,* a tower defense game that's wildly popular and, while keeping the tower defense roots, is unique and different enough to be fun and engaging. It's not as easy as it was to be a runaway hit, but it's totally still doable. As the App Store grows and grows—I don't see any slowing or stopping any time soon—it's going to fall to creative PR to get your app noticed. Highlighting it at conferences, using those types of events as launch events, etc.[34]

But don't *only* target the members of the media—remember others whom you'll find in your own backyard. You'll be surprised by the promotional platforms and influence *other developers* have.

"Fellow developers are great sources of PR," Wilker remarks.

They love talking about great apps, they can appreciate someone else's hard work, and are more than happy to celebrate another's success. PR strategies will increasingly employ social media, conferences, and the network effect to spread the word. Events provide a great place to work PR magic; meeting other developers, the Tech press, [and so on]. Enhancing and growing your network.

360iDev gives me a great window to [observe] what apps are being released. Whether it's apps my speakers are releasing or, as I mentioned, apps they find worthy of talking about, I primarily hear about what's new and hot thru the network of speakers and attendees I've created around 360iDev.[35]

If you are an expert, use conferences as an opportunity to promote not only your app, but yourself and your knowledge base.

I love it when a developer reaches out to speak at 360iDev [declares Wilker]. We love doing "How'd They Build That"–type sessions, plus in the course of their application development most developers realize there's something that no one else is talking about, some aspect of development that there are no blog posts explaining. It's great to present sessions that allow developers to say, "While building X I learned this, and I'm here to share it with you."[36]

He encourages all developers to exploit the resources 360iDev has to offer:

Leveraging my event to help your PR efforts doesn't feel slimy. I love being in a position to connect people. Developers have given me promo codes that I include in the marketing of the conference. It makes my offering more interesting to people when [it's] bundled with codes for a dozen cool new apps/games in the App Store, and it immediately increases the number of people who—if they like the app or game—will talk about it.

A great example is the Game Jam held at 360iDev—a single-night, build-a-game event. Each game created that night got a good bit of press even before it was completed and delivered to the App Store. Once each app/game was completed and turned into an actual App Store Submission—something like five at this point out of twelve or so—it got even more. People talked about the apps as they were released because of where they were created and how.

The application development space isn't a vacuum. You can write code alone and never interact with the community, but you'll be far better off for being involved. Your PR efforts will only be stronger with a strong network.

Making announcements at events like 360iDev is a great way to utilize the echo chamber effect to your benefit. With so many people in one place, all tweeting and blogging the entire time, getting some love from them is easy, and your PR efforts are exponentially magnified with little to no effort, and the only cost being the price of admission.[37]

This isn't the place to be timid, he proclaims:

Participate. Don't be a bystander in the community. Unless you're already "famous," and every app you release gets "love," you need to nurture the community and your network. Support your friends, they'll support you. Reach out to anyone and everyone you can. Attend events, be visible and accessible. The tech press comes to events like 360iDev, and if you approach them nicely, they'll talk to you.[38]

If you want to launch at a conference, get in touch with the conference organizer as early as possible. Contact information is typically very accessible on the conference site and event organizers are usually very good about responding to email due to the nature of their business. But don't approach a conference organizer until you have really fleshed out what you'd like to do at the event. Organizers are very busy people and you will be better off presenting a fleshed-out plan as opposed to sheepishly mentioning that you'd like to participate in the conference "in some way."

The more creative your idea and your pitch, the more likely the event will support your launch.

How to Handle Failure

Sometimes even great angles, positioning, and media outreach won't secure placement in the press.

"*Gas Cubby* launched on November 10, 2008, and was featured in TUAW, Gizmodo, and quite a few other blogs in the first few days, then got selected as a 'Staff Pick' on the 26th," David Barnard recalls. Things seemed to be going quite well, and success was seemingly replicable, until the launch of Barnard's next app:

> In it's first thirty days in the App Store, *Gas Cubby* made $22K. Not a runaway success, but it kept things going and gave me the confidence to keep pushing forward.
>
> The launch of *Health Cubby,* my third product, was the worst of the three. It got some attention in the press, but made only $2,200 in the first thirty days. That poor launch—along with a lot of distraction in my personal life—sent *App Cubby* into a tailspin from which I almost didn't recover. But I pushed through and things turned around.[39]

As they say, *don't panic.*

Whatever you do, don't get discouraged. If you have the great app you need to succeed, then there is a market for it.

Again I say, do *not* be annoying or persistent with the media.

"Recognize that technology writers get maybe 30 iPhone app press releases in a day. It's worth it to shoot stray bullets, but don't expect a response," *Wired.com*'s Brian X. Chen reminds.[40]

CNET's Wilson Tang believes that bringing in professionals can help kickstart a poor launch:

Get a good publicist or a marketing expert! Yes, that might sound like the cheap answer—or expensive answer, depending on where you are looking from—but relationships in this industry can get you incredibly far. The right call can make or break your app, and it's best to leave that to the experts.[41]

Henry Balanon puts outreach failure in perspective:

Sometimes it's an inferior app. Sometimes it's inferior marketing. Sometimes it's just bad timing. A study guide app might be bad for June but awesome for back to school in August. Keep your relationships with the media fresh while you analyze why things failed and what you can do next time to succeed.

No doesn't mean no forever: It means no at this point in time.[42]

Lots of the apps you know and love in the App Store didn't get press coverage right off the bat. Do everything you can to launch with the best positioning, angles, and publication targets you can.

Work really hard. Media hits aren't guaranteed, but you need to remain open to publicity opportunities. You never know when your big break will come, so keep your eyes open and put yourself out there.

This was fun, wasn't it?

See, PR isn't that scary.

You can do this. Start thinking about the different components of your PR plan and you'll be surprised by how open the media is to covering your amazing app.

You built a great app, right? Now, let's tell the world about it.

Outreach Workout

Where do you find most of the information concerning the industry?

_____

_____

_____

_____

_____

_____

_____

_____

_____

Name the ten newspapers, magazines, television programs, websites, and blogs you and your associates discuss most often.

_____

_____

_____

_____

_____

_____

_____

_____

_____

Name the top five things you most like to talk about concerning apps, mobile media, and the industry.

_____
_____
_____
_____
_____
_____
_____
_____

Name five groups of people likely to buy your app.

_____
_____
_____
_____
_____
_____
_____
_____

Name ten newspapers, magazines, television programs, websites, and blogs that specifically cover the sort of thing your app will accomplish.

_____
_____
_____
_____
_____
_____
_____
_____
_____

Judging from the reports you read, which trade shows and events seem to have all the reporters in attendance?

_____

_____

_____

_____

_____

_____

_____

_____

_____

Describe your app in ten words or less.

_____

_____

_____

_____

Describe what your app does in two to three sentences.

_____

_____

_____

_____

_____

_____

_____

_____

Identify five unique "angles" that are essential or unique to your app. Describe each angle in a single sentence.

_____

_____

_____

_____

_____

_____

_____

_____

In a single sentence, state why you created your app.

_____

_____

_____

_____

_____

_____

_____

Name five ways your fans can help to spread the word about your app.

_____

_____

_____

_____

_____

_____

_____

Name five search terms that would best lead fans to your app on Twitter.

_____

_____

_____

_____

_____

_____

_____

_____

Name five things you can't talk about without being out of your league.

_____

_____

_____

_____

_____

_____

_____

Identify five key events and conferences where you would be able to network and promote both your app and yourself.

_____

_____

_____

_____

_____

_____

_____

Why did you choose those events? What will you do once you arrive?

_____

_____

_____

_____

_____

_____

_____

_____

Name the contact persons to whom you need to reach out at each event.

_____

_____

_____

_____

_____

_____

_____

_____

_____

5

Metrics and Measurement

In addition to redefining consumer behavior, the iPhone has changed the way developers and advertisers view the opportunities they have to build for mobile platforms. Because this device is fundamentally a computer in your pocket, its basic features offer significant opportunities that weren't available before to measure and understand data and usage centered around mobile applications.

Application usage can now be measured even when users are not connected to the network. This enables a huge step forward in understanding how consumers engage with mobile apps and can help developers build *better* apps.

A measurable mobile environment also means that selling advertisements into applications becomes meaningful because ad efficacy is measured holistically rather than being tied exclusively to connected app usage. This enables an entire new generation of pricing models and revenue streams for developers. When advertisers are willing to spend on a market, the entire ecosystem benefits and grows.

Even Apple has taken notice of this. In January 2010, Apple announced its acquisition of Quattro Wireless, a mobile advertising company. This was surprising to many in the mobile advertising world. Quattro wasn't considered to be at the forefront of the iPhone ad ecosystem and, as a January 4 article in TechCrunch stated, "This is wholly unfamiliar territory for Apple."[1]

It seems as if Apple did not acquire a product so much as it acquired talent: a sales force that came with established relationships with every major advertiser and agency, now equipped with the ammunition of the Apple brand name to help them close deals. Huge deals.

Today the starting price of an Apple iAd is $1 million. In the past, the biggest mobile deal I had ever personally witnessed for a rich display ad on the iPhone platform was $250,000, and that was mind-blowing at the time. In the course of one year, the mobile display advertising market has grown exponentially, only now the market has to play by Apple's rules.[2]

There are reasons why mobile ads haven't been a dominant piece of the advertising pie. Historically, it was scary for brand owners and companies to advertise in the mobile arena because the measurement component wasn't there. For developers, there was no way to know what people liked or disliked about your application once it shipped. Even on desktop apps, measurement wasn't typically a facet that was addressed. iPhone developers are different, though. Most recognize the value in understanding usage patterns and engagement times with their apps.

Mobile phones—and particularly iPhones—are very personal devices. The apps chosen, the protective cover picked, the length of time a game is played—these are all unique to the individual user. As a result, there is a one-to-one mapping between users and their devices, a characteristic that doesn't exist on other platforms. Most activities—watching television, surfing the Internet, even driving past an array of billboards—are part of a group of activities, with many distractions as part of the total experience. When a user launches an app, however, it's typically the only activity in which the user is engaged at that particular moment.

Therefore, the data that's derived—by any means possible—can be highly accurate compared to what is available in other mediums.

Considering that I spent three years of my life building an analytics company and teaching developers and advertisers all about the mobile metrics space, this chapter is especially dear to my heart. I want to make metrics seem less scary to you. The concept of analysis can seem intimidating, even out of reach for many people, but understanding the power of data will be liberating to you as a marketer.

Let's start with the basics.

What Is a Metric, and Is It Ethical?

From a practical perspective, a metric is a quantifiable unit of measurement for . . . well . . . anything. In our case, we're going to use metrics to mean a unit of measurement for *behavior*. For example, we will determine metrics for measuring marketing success or, as we say in the biz, efficacy. These are measurements such as conversion rates, click-throughs, time spent in an application, and a lot more.

Some metrics you may want to consider for your application are:

1. Length of engagement: How long—typically measured in minutes—a user is spending in your application.

2. Focused engagement: How long—typically measured in minutes—a user spends on a specific screen of your app. For instance, if you've built a game, how long do users spend on the leaderboard screen? How does this compare to how long they spend on the home screen?

3. User preference: By comparing the two previous metrics, length of engagement versus focused engagement, you can paint a picture of what your users prefer to do with your app and dedicate resources to improving the areas highly trafficked by your audience. This can help you allocate your resources better, as well as improve your product in a way that is meaningful to your user base. Spending time, money, and energy working on a feature your users never reach is a waste. You must be smart when using the metrics available to you.

4. Click-through rate: The ratio between the users who have seen a link versus those who have clicked on it. This is typically a metric used in advertising, but it can also be helpful to you as a developer when figuring out how to allocate the real estate of your app's home screen. If users are not clicking on the "Preferences" link on your home screen, maybe there's a better way to use that space for something like, say, in-app purchases that can actually generate revenue for you along the way.

5. Conversions: iTunes Connect may tell you that your application has been downloaded 100,000 times, but if only 50,000 unique UDIDs have been measured, that means half of your user base has never opened the app, or converted. You must figure out how to rectify the discrepancy either through marketing or alternative avenues like promotion.

6. Decay: This is an example of a long-term metric. Do users spend five minutes in your app for the first seven days they have it and then only thirty seconds in it after that? Do users open your app once and never return to it? These types of metrics, coupled with the others on this list, can give you a holistic overview of the state of your application.

Once we've acquired it, we're going to take this raw data and apply it to everything you've learned in the other chapters of this book. Chapters 2, 3, and 4 were about developing habits and practices necessary to reaching the audiences specific to your product. This chapter will help you gather raw data to further focus all those other efforts. Along the way, you're going to learn the lingo.

Metrics tend to be a sticky subject for developers and product managers because the act of gathering them may seem like an invasion of your users' privacy. I don't agree. In the Internet era, app users must recognize that data is being accumulated from their usage, often without permission. As long as the data you are collecting is behavioral and remains anonymous—that is, not specific, personal data about your customer—there's no problem.[3]

In many ways, as an app developer you are Big Brother. But like Spider-Man, who was warned that with great power comes great responsibility, you can possess this power without abusing it. You can use it without giving your customers a reason not to trust you.

You can program your app, using an analytics framework such as Medialets, Flurry, or Omniture, to give you the kinds of feedback you need to achieve your goals. This will be a never-ending process. The process of installing an analytics framework is typically as simple as implementing one line of code against a library in your app (ask a developer to help if you are not a coder yourself), and it usually takes no more than thirty minutes to implement. The method by which Apple allows developers on its platform to collect data may change, but you will always be gathering data. So it all boils down to how you *use* that data. You must use the material given to you by your app, or you will miss out on many exciting opportunities to advance, promote, and scale your product.

By understanding how metrics can help you, you can design your product to maximize the returns from the analytics you gather. For instance, when you launch a new feature in an update, you can create benchmarks that reveal the average time spent in your application. Then you can learn whether that feature is causing your users to stick around longer or confusing them and turning them away.

The analytics space in mobile is constantly changing. The tools you're using now might not be the tools you'll be using tomorrow. The important thing is that you're measuring and understanding your audience.

The "Evolving Success" Metrics on the App Store

The most basic metrics feedback from the App Store will provide you with the most fundamental data every developer should follow.

The mobile application space has experienced meteoric growth since the launch of the App Store, and a lot has changed over the past eighteen months in how we determine success there. These metrics will only continue to evolve. As a community we need to keep our finger on the pulse of these changes in order to grow along with the venue. Igor Pusenjak of Lima Sky notes how he followed his app, measuring its progress every step along the way:

> We felt we had a hit when we first started working on *Doodle Jump*. And again when it was ready to be submitted to Apple for approval. But then, we felt the same at those stages about a few other games of ours that did not fare so well. Honestly, I am only now starting to really feel that we have a true hit on our hands after *Doodle Jump* has been in the top 25 for almost the last six months, reached the number-one "Top Paid App" in multiple countries, and sold over one million copies.[4]

While not as specific as engagement time or click-through rate, rankings give developers something specific they can follow as benchmarks measuring success . . . and failure. "For me, that metric is breaking through the top 50 with some momentum behind it," John Casasanta of tap tap tap says.

> If an app can crack that threshold and still has some legs, then it's likely that the exposure of being in the charts will continue to carry into the top 10. We've done it with five apps that we've been involved in so far, and those apps have had well over a million sales combined.
> Most of our marketing efforts revolve around both viral campaigns and apps that are naturally viral in the sense that people love to show them off to others. So if there's a lot of buzz generated either from our promotions or the apps themselves, then I feel like we've succeeded. Since we mainly try to create hit-based apps, the bottom line is where our apps are ranking in the charts.[5]

App *ratings* are very important in a formative market like the App Store. On the Web, sites like Amazon.com and Hotels.com also experience a similar level of importance around user-generated feedback.

"As a tech journalist, I pay less attention to app rankings, as I discover a lot of apps when developers contact me about them," *Wired.com*'s Brian X. Chen remarks.

> But I do pay close attention to *ratings*. Clearly, the more ratings an app has, the larger the indicator of the quality of the app. I've seen a lot of apps with a small number of five-star ratings, and it's obvious when those reviews are submitted by the developer's friends and colleagues—i.e., sockpuppeting—in an effort to lure people into downloading. Sometimes it works, but for the most part consumers are smart enough to discern bogus reviews from legitimate ones.
>
> The apps with high ratings from a large number of users tend to be the highest quality, and in turn they continue to sell well over a long term.[6]

"In the early days of the App Store, it was like the Wild West," Jirbo CEO Jonathan Zweig recalls.

> It was a complete land-grab situation. We were lucky enough to have fifteen applications at launch and they were downloaded by the millions. Today it's a much different environment. In order to get visibility you need to be able to target your downloader with laser-like accuracy or you are wasting your valuable marketing dollars.[7]

The unknowns keep piling up. Which apps will maintain their leads? What will consumers choose as more and more applications become available? Smart developers have been tracking their trajectory in this ecosystem, and these will establish the benchmarks by which we measure success.

The Importance of Metrics in Marketing

Metrics and data analysis around software usage may not have historically interested mobile developers on a broad scale, but now even nonbelievers are staffing up to understand the intricacies of the usage patterns around their apps.

"We haven't done much with metrics up to this point," John Casasanta admits.

> For me personally, I'd rather be spending my time working on cool UIs and thinking of fun ways to promote our apps, so I haven't gotten involved much with any form of metrics. That being said, I do think they could be important, so we very recently hired someone to help us along those lines.[8]

Atimi is a Vancouver-based software development company where cofounder and vice president Scott Michaels takes their involvement in metrics much further:

> At Atimi, measurement and metrics are part of every application launch strategy, and it is a huge red flag for us when a client does not share that vision. This is not to mean they miss the point of metrics, but the most common case is treating analytics as a secondary item when marketing, rather than the end judge of the efforts that are applied.
>
> Even for applications that are brand extensions that will be free and carry no overt ads to generate revenue, measuring what works and what did not is critical to changing marketing spends on the fly. In mobile you have that ability, whereas if you look at more traditional models the turnaround is so much slower. What is the direct impact to running a full-page ad in *Vogue* for a clothing company? That is very hard to measure, or even react to. However being able to see within an application the downloads and which pieces from

a collection are getting all the attention should absolutely trigger a change in your spending in both traditional and digital marketing efforts.

If the clothing item [you are selling] is not getting attention in the app then replace the contents of the traditional *Vogue* ad with one that is working as fast as you can.[9]

James Keller, vice president of User Experience and Strategy at development shop Small Society, has developed many well-known apps for brands such as Starbucks, Zipcar, and the Barack Obama campaign. She echoes the sentiment:

Generally speaking most of us have limited resources—either money, or time, if not both. Metrics are critical when marketing, because without them it is impossible to know if your time [or] money is being well spent. Solid metrics that are revisited on a regular basis will help you evaluate your activities and make better decisions moving forward—both with short-term tweaks to optimize your efforts, as well as providing data points that will help you develop a longer-term strategy.

I wish I could say that it should be obvious to figure out what's working for you when marketing an iPhone app, but it very well may not be. That's actually why metrics are so important. If you set your marketing benchmarks up front, and make sure to revisit them formally on a regular basis, you will have an objective way to gauge what's working and what's not.[10]

Small Society's founder, Raven Zachary, includes metrics and data analysis from the very beginning of client engagements:

As part of the discovery process with our clients, we identify the primary and secondary objectives for the app, as well as the key performance indicators—KPIs. Essentially, why you are building the app and how you will determine if it's a success in the market. KPIs may include the number of app downloads, revenue generated, repeat usage, the number of press mentions, or any number of things. These vary from project to project.

During the first six months in late 2008, you could argue that the App Store was a marketing channel. Visibility in the app store was much easier when the number of apps was smaller. Findability was less of a challenge. The App Store, first and foremost, is a distribution channel. [But] developers need to market an app off-store. App marketing takes time and money, and while there are ways to market an app frugally, you're competing for limited consumer attention with a considerably large number of app developers now.

Cash and cleverness can go a long way.[11]

Zachary finds there is a specific set of metrics that measure the success of an app:

The three data points that get the most attention are the number of downloads, revenue, and the five-star scale app rating. Only the app rating is visible to the public. On occasion, an app developer will release download and revenue numbers on a blog entry or press release to celebrate their success. Apple provides the number of downloads and revenue to a developer, but if you want greater depth, you will need to integrate an analytics solution into your app.

Longer term, I think the significance of download numbers diminishes and sustained usage over time, time spent in-app, and unique users become key metrics. Sustained usage answers the question "Have I built an app that provides long-term value in the market?" You'd be surprised how many people download an app and actually never use it. When we compare download numbers provided by Apple with unique users in our analytics data, there is a noticeable gap between the two.

In the early days of the Web, the focus was on the number of "hits" for a website. This was a poor metric for comparison between sites as it included the total number of objects downloaded on a page. If a Web page included twenty images, the hits for that page would be higher than a competing page with less images. At some point, the market matured and we moved to unique visitors and page views as the accepted metrics. This made comparisons between sites easier.

While we don't have quite the same issue on the App Store, I think there is perhaps too great of an emphasis placed upon the number of app downloads as the metric to compare apps. Free and paid apps have considerably different app download numbers—free apps are downloaded considerably more. For free apps, app downloads is a more relevant metric for comparison, while for paid apps, I'd argue that revenue is the most significant.

The top *grossing* paid app is a bigger winner than the top *downloaded* paid app.[12]

Jeff Weiser, vice president of Strategy and Analytics for Social Gaming Network (SGN)—one of the most downloaded app developers on the platform—uses data to understand where to spend money acquiring customers:

We consider metrics paramount in allocating marketing spend because they provide the basis for ROI (return on investment) assessment. If revenue from marketing activities does not exceed costs, the strategy is ill advised. We are quick to try just about anything—but equally quick to kill an initiative if early results are not demonstrably positive. Rapid iteration is the key to sustainable strategy. Most of our marketing targets user acquisition, so CPI (cost per install) most be lower than user LTV (lifetime value), which is determined by percent of users spending, ARPPU (average revenue per paying user), and churn rate.

The metrics are all important. But I'm occasionally skeptical of overreliance on gameplay metrics, for example average session time and count-of-page views. If data mining techniques reveal those metrics to be predictive of spend, that's great, but it's dangerous to make an a priori assumption that they are.[13]

"Constantly mine your own app's data," Jonathan Zweig of Jirbo advises. "Analyze and reanalyze your engagement data trends, your repeat usage, what happens when you change creative, what happens when you change the icon, etc. This can make all the difference."[14]

"There are three main things we look for at Atimi to judge the success of any given marketing campaign, that are common across all application types," Scott Michaels explains.

[They are]:

1. Total sales—or just downloads in the case of free
2. User retention levels over updates
3. Daily/weekly/monthly unique retained users of the application

Beyond this list the data points in high review are those that are specific to the actions you are looking to encourage within the application, such as conversion rates from free to paid content, or having the user drill down to some portion of the app that defines the success—such as data capture of some type.

A challenge I am sure everyone comes across when marketing an iPhone app is the very obvious fact that your efforts in the campaign can measure, say, the clickthroughs to the app store which have the expectation of becoming customers. However, your ability to measure stops there, as Apple does not provide you with stats on the conversion rate of any ability to track that the user completed the transaction to purchase the app. So you are trying to look at a mean average to work from as a baseline set of numbers. On a normal day I do "X" in sales, and now I exert new force, see result "Y."

So, you need to work from a baseline in your metrics then look at the external forces you are exerting to see the delta change in your total sales. You must also be diligent at looking at any media coverage you are getting that appears in the same timeframe [in which] you are measuring that conversion rate, as that can really skew your results. You might have written a digital campaign that actually is bombing in terms of being a success, but the write-up on a blog like TechCrunch or TUAW is what is really fueling your download burst.

There is no way to really take out all the variables, and such is life when marketing.[15]

Measurement in an Ever-Changing Environment

For developers, one of the benefits and challenges of the App Store is its nascency. The *lack* of benchmarks provides an opportunity for savvy developers to create opportunities, but it also indicates the fleeting nature of success on the App Store. Is it challenging to do marketing in a fast-paced environment?

"It is a challenge," Small Society's Raven Zachary admits.

An app's newness only lasts for one or two weeks. The best time to market an app is during that initial launch period before people's attention turns elsewhere. Compelling apps will be sustained through word-of-mouth, good reviews, and press coverage, but you have to do everything you can in that first one or two weeks to gain as much attention as possible before the next shiny app comes along. This is most pronounced in the games segment, but it is an issue throughout the iPhone app market. Sometimes luck can make or break an app's success—being featured by Apple, a well-placed press mention, or an endorsement over Twitter by someone with a large number of followers.

Everything I learn about app marketing seems to change every six months or so. We're becoming more sophisticated when it comes to marketing our iPhone apps and we're learning from the success of others. Eighteen months ago, none of us knew how to market apps. We're starting to figure this out, but it's constantly evolving as the market matures. That said, people who understand marketing's best practices have a distinct advantage over those who do not.

Some people are good marketers, some people are not. If you're not, find someone who is or resources to learn from.[16]

"Marketing in the fast-paced world of the App Store is not any more challenging than other products," Scott Michaels states.

What it takes is a more concentrated effort and the ability to be agile about the marketing you are doing and continually try, refine, push out a campaign, measure it, and start again. The intensity is certainly higher as you are doing all of those steps in a shorter amount of time than, say, for a desktop product, but it's also to your advantage as you can turn faster when the money is not being spent wisely and direct it to the next campaign method.[17]

Jirbo's Zweig has his own formula for success:

Having a successful app is 50 percent targeting, 25 percent timing, 25 percent innovation. Some of the most successful apps we've had were more about targeting and timing than anything else. This is a lesson for all developers. If you wait a year to put out your dream app, that void may be filled before you have a chance to get into that niche.[18]

SGN's Weiser sees the landscape in broad strokes:

Marketing in a fast-paced environment is less challenging than time-intensive," he says. "We're constantly monitoring the market to be sure we're the first to identify and adapt to a change.[19]

John Casasanta shares a similar viewpoint:

Sure, it can be challenging, but that just adds to the fun and excitement! If it was easy, it'd be boring. We carefully assess each situation and try to come up with new and innovative ways to promote our apps. Just because something worked once, doesn't guarantee that it will again, especially since the market is evolving so rapidly.

I've found that one of the most effective ways is to simply study the App Store itself. See what apps are selling well. Things seem to be cyclical in the App Store, so if something was selling really well at one point but then died out, there's a good chance that it, or something like it, will be selling well again in the future.

The key is to drastically improve on the past.[20]

Fundamental Market Research

"The cheapest and most effective thing to do is a basic competitive analysis," Small Society's James Keller states.

Identify at least three to five primary competitors in the marketplace who have like-minded mobile offerings for their customers. Download their apps, understand what they do, and try to ascertain why the developer made choices around feature set and approach. Make an honest effort at using the apps for an extended period of time, not just flipping through the screens. Look at the reviews and ratings from customers and understand what the primary likes and dislikes are.

Also, look for social media coverage of the competitive set, and if they were covered by the press upon launch. It is important to understand the bar that has been set by your competitors, and also to learn from mistakes that they have made. You may also be pleasantly surprised at what market data may be readily available to you by doing a little research on the Web. Make sure you take the time to search for recent industry reports or articles.

Lastly, it is also beneficial to spend the time to connect with people within your target market. This will take on a very different shape depending on the type of app you are working on—if it's a business-focused app, try joining the local chapter of a professional organization and attend a few meetings. If you are creating an app for knitters, hang out at a local yarn shop during a "stitch and bitch." If you are creating an app for kids, throw a family BBQ for friends, and do some informal Q&A with both the kids and their parents. Meeting folks can not only help you with app persona development, usability testing, beta testing, and feature prioritization for future releases—but [it] will also be able to give you hints about how different marketing channels that may be effective, how they heard about other apps that they use, and give you insight into app purchasing behaviors, pricing thresholds, and other interesting data.[21]

This approach makes use of many of the steps you took in earlier chapters and will put you ahead of other developers who may be approaching the marketplace today.

Atimi's Scott Michaels says:

I find it shocking how many people we have worked with that have not done the most basic research when entering the iPhone market, which is to search for similar applications already on the App Store,

BlackBerry's App World and Android Marketplace, download them and really get a sense of the competition. This takes very little time to do, and you should also be looking at the competitor efforts from a costing perspective on how much you think it took in real world dollars for them to develop what is there.

From there, it depends on the application, being very aware of the bigger players in your space. Just because they are not there now, don't assume. Do the following exercise in your head. If [main competitor or more prominent trusted brand] enters the app market, what will you do? Assuming they *will* enter the market, how are you going to differentiate yourself? You have to do this even before the threat exists, as somewhere in a room that looks just like yours, another team is working on something scarily similar to [what you are developing].

So to research your own market is pretty traditional market research methods.

- Trade journals
- Online
- Knowing or being a content/contextual expert in the space your app is serving

Calling [those]would-be customers and explaining your application to them. Would they buy it? Would they pay a hundred dollars for it? Two dollars? What can I do to make you agree to pay twenty dollars?[22]

"We spend a lot of time analyzing performance in the App Store," Jeff Weiser reveals.

It's less about SGN finding customers than about facilitating discovery so they can find us. The importance of visibility in the iTunes App Store cannot be overstated. Success in the iPhone market is not zero-sum, so we actually collaborate on best practices with other developers we admire.[23]

Benchmarking

Thus, in order to establish benchmarks appropriate to your app, you need to take specific steps.

As in any new market, when there are not clear metrics defined for success, the market dictates its interpretation of success itself. In the first six months of the App Store, reaching the millionth download was seen as a clear differentiator between amateur and professional app developers. At that time, there were far fewer applications competing for the space and positioning statements were much more clearly defined.

Nowadays, even reaching 500,000 downloads is seen as a success, indicating the shift in expectations from the market as it grows and matures.

Interestingly, there have never been more devices in the market, and there are still cases where an app is released and reaches the million-download mark within a matter of days. The opportunity is still real and growing, but the benchmarks for traction in the market are easing up a bit. This can be good news for you, but—once again—you must remember that your app needs to be great from the start to compete against the hundreds of thousands out there.

In an attempt to gauge the new benchmarks for success from the media's perspective, I asked TechCrunch's MG Siegler if the App Store is too crowded for 1 million-plus to be the benchmark for a runaway hit.

"Not yet," he replied, "But it's getting there. If this holiday season is any indication, the App Store is not slowing down at all, and with more apps available, the bar is going to keep being raised."[24]

"Once you decide the metrics that are important, you need to set a reasonable goal," Small Society's Keller shares.

Unfortunately, "reasonable" is often an elusive notion. The developer community, to date, has been fairly quiet in sharing their own metrics, but doing research to find the few that have, or talking one on one to other developers can certainly get a start. As much as is possible, it's nice to know what others have experienced so you can understand how your app stacks up.

Of note, however, if you are looking at the successes of other apps, make sure they are similar to your own in some way. For example, a productivity app about a niche hobby—sailing, for example—cannot be compared to a game. Also, generally speaking, an app from an independent developer will need more modest benchmarks than apps that have brand power behind them.

In lieu of data from others, the best thing you can do is set modest benchmarks based on a gut feeling, and revise your own benchmarks as often as possible once you have your own data to work with. At the end of the day, benchmarks are about optimizing your own success, and doing the best you can with your own limited set of resources. You need both quantitative and qualitative data to make sense of the larger picture, and it is important to bring the two together in a meaningful way. Generally speaking quantitative data—e.g., number of Twitter mentions—will give you a clear picture of what, while qualitative data—sentiment within those mentions—will help you answer *why*.

For example, it's not simply enough to know or track that your app is talked about on Twitter five times an hour, because if four out of five mentions simply state that the app is a failure, those mentions could be a negative, not a positive to your larger campaign.[25]

And Scott Michaels tells us:

I expect many people will discuss the number of apps in regards to benchmarking the ecosystem. At Atimi, we focus more on the quality of the application and what it is going to take to break into the top 100, top 50, top 25 and the all important 10 in any category on the app store. Part of looking at the changes is when you do your review of the new variations within a category that you need to compete with to break into the top numbers. For example the "Lifestyle" category has all types of applications that have nothing to do with the vertical or content or whom you feel would be direct competition. However, all of those apps must be on your list as perceived competitors, as you need to beat them to win each hard spot on the top 100 as your app climbs the ranks.

A real-world mechanism is to apply what you know from your own research on the costs of marketing your application. Review the real and perceived competitors in your category and come up with a best guess as to what you think they spent in development, and marketing. Double that total, because you will be guessing low. That will give you the estimated budget you will need to apply in order to earn your spot—to go along with your very competent application programming and novel concept, of course. You will find, with very few exceptions the dollar value will rise as you near the top 10 in every category.

Marketing in the iPhone ecosystem has changed in the sheer amount of money in marketing and development that it now takes to win a category on the App Store.[26]

Even Scott Michaels admits that the lack of data relating to the Store can create a daunting set of challenges to overcome:

Figuring out how to determine benchmarks is a tough question, as most applications entering the space will not have the advantage of a backlog of other applications to look to for benchmark numbers for downloads or conversion rates from free to paid. If the customer of ours has a website, we often start there with the ad spending to acquire new visitors, and then translate that to number of expected downloads to create a benchmark for the iPhone customer base. Of course, you need to temper those numbers by the particular client—by demographics how many users of the site have an iPhone?

Well, the Web analytics from the website will tell you that, so start there.[27]

"We benchmark against both our own historical performance and observable data from the market at large by giving a lot of foresight to which data elements we capture," SGN's Weiser explains.

My rule of thumb is "if you don't know how you'll use a metric to make a future decision, don't bother to record it." iPhone developers have the privilege of marketing in a data-rich environment so I encourage them to take advantage of that. The most important guideline is to maintain clarity of focus—narrow the scope of data capture and analysis to the metrics that enable informed decision-making.[28]

Making Data Actionable

My advice to developers and entrepreneurs using data to drive decision making for the first time is pick someone on the team to be solely responsible for metrics and analysis around the mobile program. The person you choose may not be the obvious choice, either. For example, your VP of Marketing may be the best person to analyze the patterns and stack them up against outreach initiatives.

But what if there *are* no other members on your team? Never fear—solo developers can use this advice, as well. Set aside at least thirty minutes a day to look over data and metrics and examine the patterns being formed.

Then determine what it is you're going to *do* with the data.

"There are two key components to making data actionable: regular analysis of the data to give it context and meaning, and then taking the time to plan and execute," James Keller says.

> It's not enough to create a great dashboard with all of the critical stats at your fingertips; you need to *work* with the data, make some assumptions, tweak your plan, reset your benchmarks, execute and re-measure. Great marketing is a painfully iterative process that when done well, takes time and attention.
>
> I would advise people to make sure to put aside the time to plan, execute and iterate—this approach makes sense for both marketing *and* for building the app itself. Even if you handle these things informally, it is important to outline a process for yourself. For building an app, once you release v1.0 into the world, you have an amazing data set that should help you organically grow your app and nurture your user base. Use tap analytics and download metrics as a basic quantitative data set, and use social media monitoring and app store rating and reviews as your qualitative set. When you bring those two sets of data together, if you still have questions, try surveying users or do usability testing to fill in the blanks. For marketing, you have different sets of data, but the plan, execute and iterate process remains the same.[29]

As mentioned earlier, the process never ends . . .

"Track everything," Scott Michaels advises.

> Every single thing that you are doing in your marketing campaign should be measurable. If it's not, why are you doing it? I am sure you don't have unlimited amount of funds so doing spends on any idea that you may come up with that can't be measured likely isn't going to provide you the data you need to transform that idea and make those same marketing dollars or human-hours of effort be less on the next round. Simple real actionable items are to use a URL

shortener such as bit.ly, and use a different one for each type of digital campaign you do in order to see the click-rate effectiveness of each one. If you are marketing a major update then what are the "type 7" downloads in iTunes Connect telling you regarding your version update/customer retention numbers?[30]

When using data to understand advertising metrics around customer acquisition, don't forget the basics.

"Fundamentally, like other forms of marketing, it's essential that you do whatever possible to isolate the affects of the various components of your marketing mix—so that you can do more of what works and less of what doesn't," advises Jamie Wells, former director of mobile for media buying agency Prometheus (Omnicom) and current director of Global Trade Marketing for Mobile Advertising Solutions at Microsoft.

For instance, executing a well-planned PR, social, and blogger outreach program in advance of any paid media will give you a good benchmark of how earned media tactics perform against specific KPIs like "downloads," "installs," "loads per month (per UU)," and "time spent per session." Once you've established your "earned media" performance benchmarks, and activity begins to fall off—standard online buzz trackers or even Google Insights can guide your sense of your app's "brand volume"—it's time to roll out the paid media campaigns.

On-device display-and-search media from mobile publishers and ad networks like Microsoft, Yahoo!, Google, AdMob and Quattro are a great place to start, as you can target users using the device that your app runs on—e.g., target media to iPhone browse or in-app to promote an iPhone app, etc. With these channels campaign performance can be directly measured to your app KPIs, so long as you install the "ad tracker" API into your app prior to launch. "Ad tracking" APIs/SDKs are supplied by many on-device mobile media providers. This will allow you to fine-tune—"optimize"—your on-device media campaign to punch up the highest performing placements, creative executions, and keyword bids—or simply keep track of ad creative burnout.

And don't forget tried-and-true marketing effectiveness methods like incentive-driven surveys. A quick "tell us how you heard about us—clicked on a banner, heard from a friend, read about online, etc.—survey" upon initial launch, along with an incentive such as a sweepstakes entry or free "X" can go a long way in isolating the effectiveness of the various elements of your app's marketing mix.[31]

Atimi's Scott Michaels advises caution, though, especially for small houses:

The best advice I can give would be to realize that you can't be both developing and marketing your application at the same time to any real level of effectiveness if you are a single to small team of developers. For larger companies who can do both, that means you have already in a sense made it to the next level. For everyone out there starting up, put into your planning that once your app is ready, your job is to *market* the application, not develop it. Put down the compiler, and put on your headset and start making calls, writing blog posts about the industry you are launching your application into, and make yourself 100 percent available for media (who are not patient; they will move on if you don't respond quickly enough) and commit yourself to writing a hundred emails a day and at least fifty phone calls to get your app at least onto the radar of the general public.

Use the measurable data from your campaign and focus on the one number that matters, reducing the overall cost of acquiring new customers to as close to zero as you can.[32]

Metrics Workout

How do your customers use your application?

_____

_____

_____

_____

_____

_____

_____

_____

_____

How can you measure their behavior?

_____

_____

_____

_____

_____

_____

_____

_____

_____

What would help you understand your audience better?

_____

_____

_____

_____

_____

_____

_____

_____

_____

Are there any specific data points that can help you understand them?

_____

_____

_____

_____

_____

_____

_____

_____

Do you have a dedicated person on your team to review metrics? Why were they chosen for this role?

_____

_____

_____

_____

_____

_____

_____

_____

How often do you plan on reviewing statistics around your application?

_____

_____

_____

_____

_____

_____

_____

_____

_____

How would you like to see your metrics evolve over time?

_____

_____

_____

_____

_____

_____

_____

_____

_____

How can you use your app to drive engagement for users with your app? (For example, push notifications reminding users there is new content, social media tie-ins such as sending high scores to Twitter, etc.)

_____

_____

_____

_____

_____

_____

_____

_____

_____

6

The Never-Ending Story

Well, friends, we've made it. The final chapter. Or so it seems . . .

It's not the end of your journey, really, but it's the light at the end of the tunnel. And this chapter is the toughest chapter of all, for many reasons—especially because while there are no set metrics for success, by this point you need to be establishing *your own* parameters.

It's entirely up to you.

Everyone's outcome after reading this book will be different. It will depend on the work you've done in the previous chapters, combined with the strength of your idea, the quality of your app, and the circumstances of your launch. There's no right or wrong, no winning or losing. Your expectations are your own—both for your app and for what you're looking to get out of *Mobilize*—and only you can know if and when you've achieved the success you're looking for.

So now you've come to understand the components necessary for launching and building a brand on the App Store. You've:

- Lined up your launch publicity
- Instrumented your app to retrieve analytic data
- Polished your messaging
- Submitted your app for approval

Now you wait patiently while Apple's employees scour your app for bugs and whatever else the team in Cupertino, California, looks for in making the determination as to whether or not your app is worthy of assuming a place in the App Store.

If all goes well and there are no problems, this process should take less than seven days—at least according to Apple's press releases. Apple loves to trumpet its fast turnaround in app approvals, touting a 95 percent conversion of apps, from submission to listing on the App Store, within a week.

While many use Apple's clandestine policies as reason to predict that open platforms like Android will win in the end, the reality is that seven days isn't very long to wait to enter the planet's most robust mobile application marketplace. Hundreds of thousands of developers agree.

Regardless, many developers use the possibility of being rejected by Apple as a reason to avoid building an app in the first place. But that's just an excuse for not having the guts to try. The fact is that unless an app has broken a known rule or harbors nefarious intent, Apple does not for the most part want to deny applications the opportunity to be listed in its store. Think about it. The more applications in the store, the more variety of content Apple can offer, the more hardware it will sell.

At the end of the day, Apple is a hardware company.

These apps—including yours—are helping to sell iPods and iPhones and iPads. Apple understands this, and you should as well.

First and Foremost . . .

There are a lot of great books on the market, some of which I will list under the suggested readings. They describe in great detail how to go through the actual technical steps of getting your app listed on the App Store, as well as how to upload binaries, how to assign promo codes, and so forth. But *Mobilize* focuses on the marketing aspects of the process. Now that you've stuck around till the end (and aren't you glad you did?) I'm going to give you the best piece of advice you'll find in the entire book.

> When you submit your app to Apple, be sure to list your launch date as taking place at least a month after you intend to launch.

I see it time and time again. Developers work excruciatingly hard, crafting their product, detailing a launch plan, getting materials together and scheduling interviews, only to have their launch window devastated by poor planning.

If at the end of the development process you upload your application to Apple for approval, saying you want to launch a week from that day, then when your app gets approved on that day it will *immediately* be listed in the App Store. This allows you no time whatsoever to execute the launch-day plans upon which so much of your PR and marketing are based.

The result is a hugely wasted opportunity.

On the other hand, if you state your date for sometime in the future and your app is approved, you can always edit your launch details through iTunes Connect and set the date for sooner. This gives you some modicum of control over your launch and enables you to plan well and execute effectively.

Be a Watchful Parent

Once your app is launched, keep a close eye on your metrics. Understand how users are reacting to your product and watch the category lists to see where you rank compared to others in your space. If you've done an exceptional job with your launch PR, you may have ascended to the top 100 apps. It's your responsibility to do all you can to stay there. We have already talked about the benefits of being on the top lists in the App Store, as well as the network effects that come along with those plum spots.

If you *haven't* hit a spot in the top 100, then use every trick in the book—this book, of course—to try to get there.

But even if you launch at number one in the App Store, your work is just beginning.

This chapter is called "The Never-Ending Story" because that's what marketing is: a continuous cycle of evaluation and execution. You must be keenly aware of everything surrounding your product—publicity, download counts, rankings, public sentiment, competitors, and so much more. Additionally, you must have your finger on the pulse of what's happening in the marketplace, so you can adapt and adjust to it and maintain or even enhance your position in your category.

Think about your favorite websites. Whether it's the content or the design, they are constantly changing. Upgrading. Keeping you interested.

Your app is the same. It will not refresh itself on its own, and leaving it to stagnate simply isn't an option, not if you want to achieve long-term success. Think about many of the apps from just two years ago. They look so antiquated compared to the apps being released now. The same will be true of your application. By 2015, an app from 2012 will look like a cave painting.

You must keep up with the current design trends and the best practices of the ecosystem you're selling in. You must be *proactive.*

This has to be a priority engrained in the DNA of your development cycle.

By the same token, don't simply redesign for the sake of appearing busy. Everything you do must be done with a defined purpose in mind. There have to be clear business objectives behind all your efforts. For instance, if your content is stale, or the design doesn't reflect the current state of the industry, you will lose the competitive edge you've fought so hard to achieve. *That's* when you need to get it into gear.

Don't change things that are working, but constantly seek to stay on the cutting edge of what's happening in this space.

T-Minus Launch and Counting

If you've done everything properly, this is what you've got going for you:

- Understanding of the market
- Positioning statement
- Marketing objectives
- Marketing plan
- Outreach plan
- Key metrics defined

If you can check off all of those bullet points, it's all in place. You're ready for action.

It's up to you to remember all these components, stick to them, and execute. If you've assessed your market opportunity well, it's going to continue into perpetuity. After all, the purpose of this book is to teach you how to *build* a brand on the App Store, not strike it rich quick, then get out of the game.

This is a marathon, not a sprint.

Set your expectations correctly. You have to be honest with yourself about what you're able to do given your budget, team size, marketing resources, PR experience, and a host of other components critical to launching a product. Maintain an exhaustive list of all of the goals you want to achieve with your launch, then create a second list of what you would be satisfied with. Work toward completing the first, all-inclusive list, then check it against the second list to ensure that at the very least your baseline objectives are being met.

Think critically about your product when making these assessments. Are you *Halo* or are you *Asteroids?* One isn't necessarily better than the other—each has a completely different set of goals and objectives. A high-budget, low-profit margin game may seem shiny and exciting, but it may not deliver the value you expect. So just because you're *Asteroids* doesn't means that you can't sell a boatload of copies.

Many of the top applications in the App Store have won their position because they knew what they were meant to be. *Doodle Jump,* a simple and inexpensive game, has been at the top of the charts as long as I can remember because the team there never tried to be something they're not. As long as you've properly defined your product within the market, you may find that your app is better suited as a simple $0.99 game than a $20 mammoth title that intends to take on the major game publishers.

At the end of the day, the iPhone is still viewed by many as an entertainment platform, and "more expensive" does not always mean "better." Be true to what you want to build and your customers will be receptive.

What I've provided you in this book is a template for launching an app in the App Store and how to engage in the new mobile ecosystem. If you follow this, you've exponentially increased your likelihood of success. It's not to say that you cannot find your own way of launching—in fact, I encourage that—but these are the basal components necessary to competing on par with your rivals in the App Store.

More important, if you *don't* follow this template, you will have severely limited your possibilities of success.

If It's Working . . .

Congratulations!

If you're achieving the results you were looking for immediately after you launch, that's a very exciting sign. However, even if it's working, it has to continue to work. You must be able to sustain your growth. Once you've launched your app, the real work begins.

Remember, you're building a business here. Sustainability and steady growth are critical. Your app sales are fragile. You need to check them, track them as short-term trends, and track them regularly as long-term trends.

So how do you follow these trends? Think back to chapter 5. Based on what we covered in that chapter, you should have in place the metrics appropriate to determine the processes and success parameters for your specific app and for your particular business. The trick to using this data in a meaningful way is to avoid getting caught up in the actual figures, and start thinking critically about ways to transition it into actionable shifts for your business. You'll truly begin to appreciate metrics when you get to the point where hard data indicates you're doing something that could be improved by making not massive changes, but slight adjustments.

If It's Not Working . . .

Fear not.

While we've seen huge leaps in the adoption of this platform, bear in mind that we're still in the very early stages of the App Store and in the midst of tremendous growth. As long as you're willing to be open-minded, looking for ways to change your situation, then a lackluster launch won't be the end of the world.

Nor is it the end of your career as an app developer on the iPhone platform.

If your launch failed and you *still* want to stay in this business, the key is to determine what happened. The most important thing you can do is to be supercritical about what occurred.

- Was it the product?
- Was it that you couldn't find the audience?
- Was it that your product was leapfrogged?
- Did someone do something that blindsided you?

Some of these things you can't do a thing about. In those cases, you must evaluate the level of effort required to recover, then determine whether or not what happened is irrevocable.

On the other hand, there may still be things you can learn from failure, perhaps to the point of turning it around.

- What have the reviews told you?
- What have the sales told you?
- What have the analytics told you?
- What do you do next?

You must figure out what went wrong if you don't want it to happen again. And to do that . . .

Rinse . . . and Repeat

How many times have we said it? Now that you've gone through all of the steps, read all of the chapters, done all of the exercises—do it all again.

Give the book to everyone on your team, too. Make them do it all again. If you're dealing with problems, you'll find a way to deal with them. And if everything's going well, then you'll find a way to make it go even better. The fact is that the answers you supply in the workout sections before the launch will be vastly different than the answers you give six months into your product's lifespan.

This is good news!

It means you are growing and evolving along with the market. This is the key to building a *business,* not just throwing something out to see if it sticks.

But do it your way. Don't just read about mobilization. *Become* mobilization. "Mobile" does not just have to be the platform you've built your product upon. *Mobilize* your fan base. Get people *excited.* You've built a great app, right?

Now, shout it from the rooftops.

By this point you've got the concept of mobilization woven into every facet of your thought processes, your development processes, your stages of execution. But you should *never* do it slavishly, adhering rigidly to anyone else's model—even mine.

Become an evangelist, and establish yourself as an expert. If all goes well, the next edition of this book will be quoting *you,* describing everything you did to make your app a genuine killer.

Thinking two steps ahead: that's the secret to long-term success on the front lines of the app revolution.

Glossary

App A program that runs on an iPhone, iPod Touch, or iPad.

App Store Apple's marketplace for distributing apps.

API (application programming interface) An interface developed to provide access from one software program to other software. An example of the use of an API is Google Maps integration in *foursquare.*

Cocoa An application program environment, available for Mac OS X, that enables developers to create apps using tools provided by Apple as well as other third-party tools.

Disintermediation The removal of third parties in a process, a.k.a. "taking out the middle man."

J2ME (Java 2, micro edition) A Java-based platform designed for mobile devices ranging from pagers and mobile telephones through set-top boxes and car navigation systems.

Mind share A measure of customer awareness of a business or brand relative to its competitors. Capturing mind share is typically the means to becoming the leader of the pack, the first step to becoming synonymous with the brand name in a category—and that's the holy grail of branding.

Multitouch display A type of touchscreen technology used on Apple devices such as the iPhone and iPad that enables users to apply multiple finger gestures simultaneously on the screen.

On deck Inclusion on a mobile device shipping to consumers; standard apps shipped with a phone.

Positioning The process of building an identity in the minds of your target market for your product or brand.

Positioning statement A statement describing how you are perceived by your customer base and the market at large.

SDK (software development kit) A framework provided by Apple for building applications on its iOS platform.

SWOT (strengths, weaknesses, opportunities, threats) An analysis tool used for determining how to market in an environment with multiple competitors.

UDID (unique device identifier) A unique code assigned to each iPhone shipped.

Virtual goods An intangible gift; nonphysical objects purchased for use in online communities.

Notes

Chapter 1

1. "Apple Reinvents the Phone with iPhone," Apple, www.apple.com/pr/library/2007/01/09iphone.html.

2. "Apple-Legal-Trademark List," Apple, www.apple.com/legal/trademark/appletmlist.html.

3. "iPhone App Store Downloads Top 10 Million in First Weekend," Apple, www.apple.com/pr/library/2008/07/14appstore.html.

4. Brian X. Chen, interview with author, November 28, 2009.

5. Lucius Kwok, email interview with author, November 28, 2009.

6. Dan Frommer, email interview with author, November 29, 2009.

7. Wil Shipley, interview with author, November 29, 2009.

8. "UIDevice Class Reference," Apple, http://developer.apple.com/iphone/library/documentation/uikit/reference/UIDevice_Class/Reference/UIDevice.html.

9. Brian Crecente, "DS Breaks 100M Sold Worldwide," Kotaku, March 11, 2009, http://kotaku.com/5167971/ds-breaks-100m-sold-worldwide.

10. Brian Ashcraft, "PSP Reaches 50 Million in Worldwide Sales," Kotaku, February 13, 2009, http://kotaku.com/5152847/psp-reaches-50-million-in-worldwide-sales; Marguerite Reardon, "New App Store Section for Premium Games?," CNET News, January 29, 2009, http://news.cnet.com/8301-13579_3-10152615-37.html.

11. Priya Ganapati, "Rumor: iPhone to Get a Premium App Store," *Wired,* www.wired.com/gadgetlab/2009/03/post/.

12. Frommer, interview with author, November 29, 2009.

13. John Markoff and Laura M. Holson, "Apple's Latest Opens a Developers' Playground," *New York Times,* July 10, 2008, http://www.nytimes.com/2008/07/10/technology/personaltech/10apps.html.

14. Dylan Stableford, "Next-Gen iPhone: Thinner, Better Battery, Video Calling," Media Alley, June 7, 2010, www.thewrap.com/media/column-post/next-gen-iphone-thinner-better-battery-video-calling-18094.

15. Peter Lee, email interview with author, November 29, 2009.

16. Kathleen McMahon, interview with author, March 3, 2010.

17. Lee, email interview with author, November 29, 2009.

18. McMahon, interview with author, March 3, 2010.

19. "Thanks a Billion," Apple, www.apple.com/itunes/billion-app-countdown/.

20. "Apple's App Store Downloads Top 1.5 Billion in First Year," Apple, www.apple.com/pr/library/2009/07/14apps.html.

21. Andrew Nusca, "Apple App Store Apps Top 2 Billion; That's 6.6 Million Downloads Per Day," ZDNet, September 28, 2009, www.zdnet.com/blog/gadgetreviews/apple-app-store-apps-top-2-billion-thats-66-million-downloads-per-day/7887.

22. "iPhone SDK Downloads Top 250,000: New App Store Available in 62 Countries," Apple, www.apple.com/pr/library/2008/06/09iphone_sdk.html.

23. Peter Kafka, "Apple: We're at 200,000 Apps and Counting. And None of Them Use Flash," All Things Digital, April 29, 2010, http://mediamemo.allthingsd.com/20100429/apple-were-at-200000-ipad-apps-and-counting-and-none-of-them-use-flash/.

24. John Markoff and Laura M. Holson, "Apple's Latest Opens a Developers' Playground," New York Times, July 10, 2008, http://www.nytimes.com/2008/07/10/technology/personaltech/10apps.html.

25. Jeff Scott, "App Store Changes Adds Keywords, Restricts Name Changes, Search May Ignore Description," 148Apps.biz, July 29, 2009, http://148apps.biz/app-store-changes-adds-keywords-restricts-name-changes-search-may-ignore-description/.

26. http://www.medialets.com/blog/2008/07/31/the-hole-in-the-wall-and-the-window-of-opportunity-from-free-to-paid-for-free-and-paid/.

27. Frommer, email interview with author, November 29, 2009.

28. Chen, interview with author, November 28, 2009.

29. Frommer, email interview with author, November 29, 2009.

30. Interview on November 28, 2009.

31. Scott Michaels, interview with author, December 3, 2009.

32. Ibid.

33. MG Siegler, "Here's How iPhone App Store Ratings Work. Hint: They Don't," TechCrunch, June 29, 2009, http://techcrunch.com/2009/06/29/heres-how-iphone-app-store-ratings-work-hint-they-dont/.

34. Michael Essany, "iPhone 4.0 Dumps 'Rate on Delete' for Apps," Modmyi.com, April 11, 2010, http://modmyi.com/forums/iphone-news/706339-iphone-4-0-dumps-rate-delete-apps.html.

35. Mark Milian, interview with author, November 29, 2009.

36. Kit Eaton, "iPhone Owners Spend More Money—and Not Just on Apple Hardware," Fast Company, November 25, 2009, www.fastcompany.com/blog/kit-eaton/technomix/hey-big-online-spender-you-must-be-iphone-owner.

37. "Apple Sells Two Million iPads in Less Than 60 Days," Apple, www.apple.com/pr/library/2010/05/31ipad.html.

38. Brian X. Chen, "Coder's Half-Million-Dollar Baby Proves iPhone Gold Rush Is Still On," *Wired,* February 12, 2009, www.wired.com/gadgetlab/2009/02/shoot-is-iphone/.

39. Gagan Biyani, "Apple Bans App Store's 3rd-Most Prolific Developer," MobileCrunch, August 3, 2009, www.mobilecrunch.com/2009/08/03/apple-bans-app-stores-3rd-most-prolific-developer/.

40. Ibid.

41. Chen, interview with author, November 28, 2009.

42. Ibid.

43. Rana Sobhany, "Steve Jobs: Thoughts on Flash," The iPhone Era, April 29, 2010, http://iphoneera.com/posts/2010/3/22/apple-closing-gap-on-app-store-inadequacies.html.

44. Michaels, interview with author, December 20, 2009.

Chapter 2

1. Al Ries and Jack Trout, *Positioning: The Battle for Your Mind* (New York: McGraw-Hill, 2001), 19.

2. "Ed Catmull, Pixar: Keep Your Crises Small (with transcript)," Fearless Coder, February 25, 2010, http://fearlesscoder.blogspot.com/2010/02/ed-catmull-pixar-keep-your-crises-small.html.

3. Weldon Dodd, email interview with author, March 2, 2010.

4. Ibid.

5. Ibid.

6. Ibid.

7. Craig Hockenberry, interview with author, December 21, 2009.

8. Ibid.

9. Harry Beckwith, *Selling the Invisible: A Field Guide to Modern Marketing* (New York: Warner Books, 1997), 113.

10. "Corporate Information," Google, www.google.com/corporate/.

11. "Shazam Surpasses 50 Million Global Users and Attracts Investment from the Backers of Google and Amazon," Shazam, www.shazam.com/music/web/newsdetail.html?nid=NEWS089.

12. Kathleen McMahon, interview with author, March 3, 2010.

13. Naveen Selvadurai, email interview with author, December 21, 2009.

14. Ibid.

15. "Sustainability-Supplier Expectations," Coca-Cola Company, www.thecoca-colacompany.com/citizenship/supplier_expectations.html.

16. "Investor Relations: FAQs," Amazon.com, http://phx.corporate-ir.net/phoenix.zhtml?c=97664&p=irol-faq.

17. Bryan Duke, interview with author, December 20, 2009.

Chapter 3

1. John Vechey, email interview with author, December 20, 2009.

2. Brian X. Chen, email interview with author, November 28, 2009.

3. Igor Pusenjak, email interview with author, December 21, 2009.

4. Mark Jardine, email interview with author, December 21, 2009.

5. Kathleen McMahon, email interview with author, March 3, 2010.

6. David Barnard, interview with author, January 4, 2010.

7. Ibid.

8. Ibid.

9. Jardine, email interview with author, December 21, 2009.

10. John Casasanta, email interview with author, December 21, 2009.

11. Bryan Duke, email interview with author, December 20, 2009.

12. Ibid.

13. Ibid.

14. Matt Martel, email interview with author, December 21, 2009.

15. Ibid.

16. Selvadurai, email interview with author, December 21, 2009.

17. Vechey, email interview with author, December 20, 2009.

18. Martel, email interview with author, December 21, 2009.

19. Jason Jacobs, interview with author, December 29, 2009.

20. Casasanta, email interview with author, December 20, 2009.

21. Martel, email interview with author, December 21, 2009.

22. Adam Lisagor, email interview with author, December 30, 2009.

23. Ibid.

24. Vechey, email interview with author, December 20, 2009.

25. Pusenjak, email interview with author, December 21, 2009.

26. Jacobs, interview with author, December 29, 2009.

27. Lisagor, email interview with author, December 30, 2009.

28. Jacobs, interview with author, December 29, 2009.

29. Ibid.

30. Lisagor, interview with author, December 30, 2009.

31. Jacobs, interview with author, December 29. 2009.

32. Barnard, email interview with author, January 4, 2010.

33. Ibid.

34. Jenna Wortham, email interview with author, December 30, 2009.

35. Duke, email interview with author, December 20, 2009.

36. Ibid.

37. Colin Smith, email interview with author, December 21, 2009.

38. Vechey, email interview with author, December 20, 2009.

39. Ibid.

40. Craig Hockenberry, email interview with author, December 21, 2009.

41. MG Siegler, email interview with author on December 30, 2009.

42. Martel, email interview with author, December 21, 2009.

43. Smith, email interview with author, December 21, 2009.

44. Chen, email interview with author, November 28, 2009.

45. Matt Drance, email interview with author, January 3, 2010.

46. Ibid.

47. Ibid.

48. Ibid.

49. Jacobs, interview with author, December 29, 2009.

50. Vechey, email interview with author, December 20, 2009.

51. Barnard, email interview with author, January 4, 2010.

52. Jardine, email interview with author, December 21, 2009.

53. Pusenjak, email interview with author, December 21, 2009.

54. Casasanta, email interview with author, December 20, 2009.

55. David Barnard, email interview with author, December 20, 2009.

56. Loren Brichter, email interview with author, December 21, 2009.

57. Ibid.

Chapter 4

1. Brian X. Chen, email interview with author, December 20, 2009.

2. Jason Jacobs, email interview with author, December 20, 2009.

3. John Casasanta, email interview with author, December 21, 2009.

4. Ibid.

5. Chen, email interview with author, December 20, 2009.

6. Igor Pusenjak, email interview with author, December 21, 2009.

7. Wilson Tang, email interview with author, December 21, 2009.

8. Ibid.

9. Ibid.

10. David Lieb, email interview with author, December 21, 2009.

11. Ibid.

12. Ibid.

13. Ibid.

14. MG Siegler, email interview with author, December 30, 2009.

15. Ibid.

16. Ibid.

17. Jardine, email interview with author, December 21, 2009.

18. Ibid.

19. Ibid.

20. David Barnard, email interview with author, December 21, 2009.

21. Jason Jacobs, email interview with author, December 21, 2009.

22. Pusenjak, email interview with author, December 21, 2009.

23. Jardine, email interview with author, December 21, 2009.

24. Naveen Selvadurai, interview with author, December 21, 2009.

25. Ibid.

26. Mark Milian, interview with author, February 28, 2010.

27. Wilson Tang, email interview with author, December 20, 2009.

28. Ibid.

29. Henry Balanon, email interview with author, December 20, 2009.

30. Henry Balanon, email interview with author, December 22, 2009.

31. Ibid.

32. Bryan Duke, email interview with author, December 20, 2009.

33. Jacobs, email interview with author, December 20, 2009.

34. John Wilker, email interview with author, December 21, 2009.

35. Ibid.

36. Ibid.

37. Ibid.

38. Ibid.

39. David Barnard, email interview with author, January 4, 2010.

40. Brian X. Chen, email interview with author, November 28, 2009.

41. Tang, email interview with author, December 20, 2009.

42. Balanon, email interview with author, December 20, 2009.

Chapter 5

1. Jason Kincaid, "Denied AdMob, Apple Buys Competing Ad Platform Quattro Wireless for $275 Million," TechCruncy, January 4, 2010, http://techcrunch.com/2010/01/04/apple-acquires-quattro-wireless/.

2. Eliot Van Buskirk, "Apple iAd Platform's Entry Fee Reported to Be $1 Million," *Wired*, April 29, 2010, www.wired.com/epicenter/2010/04/apples-iad-platforms-reported-entry-fee-1-million/.

3. "Global Code of Conduct," MMA (Mobile Marketing Association) Global, http://mmaglobal.com/codeofconduct.pdf.

4. Igor Pusenjak, interview with author, January 2, 2010.

5. John Casasanta, email interview with author, December 21, 2010.

6. Brian X. Chen, interview with author, November 20, 2009.

7. Jonathan Zweig, email interview with author, March 2, 2010.

8. John Casasanta, interview with author, February 28, 2010.

9. Scott Michaels, email interview with author, February 27, 2010.

10. James Keller, email interview with author, February 28, 2010.

11. Raven Zachary, email interview with author, February 28, 2010.

12. Ibid.

13. Jeff Weiser, email interview with author, February 28, 2010.

14. Jonathan Zweig, email interview with author, March 3, 2010.

15. Michaels, email interview with author, February 27, 2010.

16. Zachary, email interview with author, February 28, 2010.

17. Michaels, email interview with author, February 27, 2010.

18. Zweig, email interview with author, March 3, 2010,

19. Weiser, email interview with author, February 28, 2010.

20. Casasanta, email interview with author, February 28, 2010.

21. Keller, email interview with author, February 28, 2010.

22. Michaels, email interview with author, February 27, 2010.

23. Weiser, email interview with author, February 28, 2010.

24. MG Siegler, email interview with author, December 30, 2009.

25. Keller, email interview with author, February 28, 2010.

26. Michaels, email interview with author, February 27, 2010.

27. Ibid.

28. Weiser, email interview with author, February 28. 2010.

29. Keller, email interview with author, February 28, 2010.

30. Michaels, email interview with author, February 27, 2010.

31. Jamie Wells, email interview with author, March 6, 2010.

32. Scott Michaels, email interview with author, March 3, 2010.

Suggested Readings

Chen, Brian X., *Always On: How the iPhone Unlocked the Anything, Anytime, Anywhere Future,* Da Capo Press, 2011.

Dudney, Bill, Writing Your First iPhone Application (screencast), http://pragprog.com/screencasts/v-bdiphone/writing-your-first-iphone-application.

Dudney, Bill, and Chris Adamson, *iPhone SDK Development,* Pragmatic Bookshelf, 2009.

Gladwell, Malcolm, *The Tipping Point,* Boston: Back Bay Books, 2002.

Hockenberry, Craig, *iPhone App Development: The Missing Manual,* http://appdevmanual.com.

LaMarche, Jeff, and David Mark, *Beginning iPhone 3 Development: Exploring the iPhone SDK,* Apress, 2009.

Ries, Al, and Jack Trout, *Positioning: The Battle for Your Mind,* McGraw-Hill, 2000.

Other Resources

Apple Outsider, Matt Drance, www.appleoutsider.com.

Daring Fireball, John Gruber, http://www.daringfireball.net.

Gadget Lab blog, *Wired. com,* http://www.wired.com/gadgetlab.

Pocket Gamer, www.pocketgamer.co.uk.

Index